GW01607957

THE ASHES

England in Australia 1990-91

Winner: Allan Border in full swing during Australia's final victory in Perth. Border's tough early days as Australian captain have been repaid in full with dramatic victories in the World Cup, and back-to-back Ashes successes over the old rival, England.

THE ASHES

England in Australia 1990-91

Mark Ray
and Alan Lee

with
David Gower
Mark Taylor
Ross Dundas
Matthew Engel

Photography by Mark Ray and Graham Morris

William Heinemann Australia

William Heinemann Australia
22 Salmon Street
Port Melbourne Victoria 3207
Australia

First published 1991
by The Text Publishing Company Pty Ltd
220 Clarendon Street
East Melbourne Victoria 3002
Australia

Designed by World of Wonders
Typeset by Text Media
Printed and bound at Griffin Press, South Australia

National Library of Australia
Cataloguing-in-Publication data:

Ray, Mark.
The Ashes: England in Australia 1990-91.

ISBN 0 85561 444 7.

1. Test matches (Cricket). I. Lee, Alan, 1954-
II. Title.

796.35865

Colour photographs by Graham Morris
Black and white photographs by Mark Ray (except photographs on pp17, 33, 36, 40, 51, 57, 66, 68, 70, 73, 75, 85, 86, 87, 92, 93, 94, 96, 104, 109, 119, 123, 148, 149 by Graham Morris)

CONTENTS

Jubilation: Australians celebrating yet another dismissal of an England batsman. This time the combination of Craig McDermott (bowler) and Ian Healy (wicket-keeper). Lending the usual support are Mark Taylor, Terry Alderman, Dean Jones, Geoff Marsh and Mark Waugh.

ALL HAIL THE AUSTRALIANS

IN THE 1989 Ashes series in England, all Australia had to do to win a Test match was give the ball to Terry Alderman, settle back in the slips and watch England's batsmen commit suicide. If Robin Smith or David Gower happened to make a few runs, it merely served to motivate Mark Taylor, Dean Jones and Steve Waugh to score more heavily than they had intended. Either way, Australia was never placed under sustained pressure, never asked to show how it would cope with decent opposition.

Whenever disaster threatened, the Australians thought calmly about what was required, then did it.

In the return series in Australia in 1990-91, Allan Border's team won 3-0 from five Tests and Graham Gooch's supposedly rejuvenated England side left with the appalling record of one first-class win from eleven matches. Yet somehow England managed to ask more questions of the Australians than it had in 1989. Different players provided the answers but, in the end, the result was the same. Perhaps even better for Australia.

After England's improved showing against the West Indies in the Caribbean, followed by series wins against New Zealand and India in England, much was expected of the tourists. Led by Gooch, England's batting seemed to have recovered from the horrors of 1989, with Allan Lamb, Robin Smith and Mike Atherton joining their captain in the 1990 run-feast. There was a suspicion in Australia that these runs had been made against friendly attacks on friendly English wickets, but there was also the suspicion that England might not find Australia's bowling as challenging as it had in 1989. In the previous domestic season, Australia had failed to bowl out New Zealand, Sri Lanka and Pakistan to win Test matches it had dominated. Alderman would not be as effective in Australia as he was in England and Gooch, especially, had risen in stature with his new responsibility as England captain.

Dismay: Craig McDermott and Terry Alderman frame David Gower as he leaves the field, unconquered but immensely frustrated at yet another England failure.

Enter from left-arm over the wicket, the two-metre-long stick-like figure of Bruce Reid. With one delivery in the first Test – a swinging yorker that clean-bowled Smith emphatically – Reid showed that he was again at his best, after two years out with a serious back injury, and that Australia had a bowler penetrative enough to cover for Alderman should he not prove as destructive as in 1989.

Reid took 27 wickets at 16 in four Tests and the pace attack took 70 of the 79 wickets to fall to Australia's bowlers. When Alderman and Reid were rested from the fourth and fifth Tests respectively, Craig McDermott took 18 wickets at 20 in those two matches. However spineless and technically deficient England's batting had been, and it was both, Australia's bowlers dominated impressively. They were supported by excellent fielding, led by wicket-keeper Ian Healy who took twenty-four catches for the series.

The best aspect of England's play was its bowling, which put Australia under more pressure than in 1989, despite a fielding team that Gooch described as the worst he had ever had the misfortune to play alongside. Thanks to England's bowling, Australia's most fancied batsmen did not prosper as expected.

Mark Taylor's effectiveness was greatly reduced by England's tactic of bowling around the wicket. With Geoff Marsh struggling at times the openers did not make life as easy for those who followed as they had in the previous series. Dean Jones and Steve Waugh both failed to make runs, though when Steve was dropped after three Tests, his twin brother Mark made a superb debut hundred, strolling into Test cricket with the ease of a veteran and confirming Australia's batting depth as McDermott confirmed the depth of its bowling.

England actually led on the first innings on two occasions but could not convert those advantages into wins, either because of second-innings collapses or excellent rearguard innings from David Boon and the Australian middle-to-lower order. At numbers seven and eight, Greg Matthews and Ian Healy played very well, and all the pace bowlers contributed runs at various times.

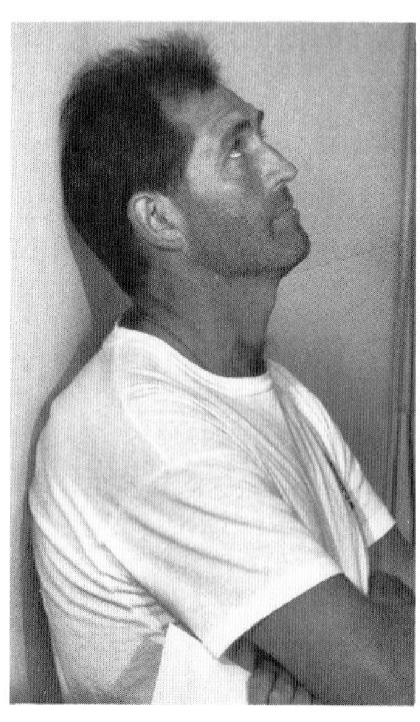

Oh me, oh my: Graham Gooch looks to the heavens for inspiration. Sorry skip, none there either.

That lower-order batting strength provided the clearest evidence of Australia's superiority. Whenever disaster threatened, the Australians took deep breaths, thought calmly about what was required, then put their heads down and did it. Whenever disaster threatened the Englishmen, they welcomed it with the readiness of players who knew deep down that they were not good enough.

What the 1990-91 Ashes series revealed about Australia was that it could rely on many more players than the few who monopolised the score-sheets in England in 1989 – and on some who were not even on that tour. The question of whether Australia had the depth and ability to continue to develop until it could lay legitimate claim to being the world's best Test team had not yet been answered, but only because England did not provide strong enough opposition. Still, whatever the quality of the opposition, in order to win, a team need only play as well as required. Australia's greater depth of talent and its ability to draw on that talent when it was needed most far surpassed that of a sadly deficient England.

Where to, England?

The English view

Alan Lee exonerates the England captain, and suggests head-hunters must look elsewhere.

THERE IS no shame in being beaten by a superior force. Shame is imposed when things might have been different, when the odds might have been upset, and when opportunities were wantonly surrendered through a lack of resilience and spirit.

This is England's humiliation at the end of this Ashes series, a series in which it failed to take a trick despite, at different stages of each game, having much the better hand. Its indictment is not only being beaten by an Australian side performing below its best, but being beaten in a manner which hinted strongly at a lack of care and devotion.

It was almost more than Graham Gooch could bear. As the tour progressed, the captain, whose commitment could never be questioned, found himself ever more horrified as the basics of the game were being flouted in batting collapses, which became as traditional a Test match feature as Tony Greig's pitch report, and in stunningly poor fielding.

There was more, though, to dismay the leader who refused to recognise a lost cause. Gooch's deeds, probably his words too, were inspirational, but there were those in his side who declined to be inspired. To Gooch, it was unthinkable and insidious that anyone could be representing England and apparently not want to give his best.

In the past, when Gooch's cricketing career has entered a crisis, his nature has been to retreat rather than confront the enemy. He has, in his time, asked to be dropped by both Essex and England when out of form. He has also given up the captaincy of Essex, later to retake it, and has taken a decision to end his touring days with England, later to be revised. Analytical and self-critical to a painful degree, there was a distinct possibility, towards the end of this tour, that Gooch would once more consider it the best and most honourable course to withdraw from a situation which, he felt keenly, he had tried but failed to correct.

Gooch considered resignation. It may only have crossed his mind in the bleakest of depressions, but he admits it was an option. Then, thankfully, he delivered himself of the notion, not only because he was constantly being told there was nobody to replace him but because captaincy is a vocation he relishes.

As the players left Australia, heading mournfully for New Zealand and a three-match series of one-day internationals for which few can have felt any genuine enthusiasm, their futures, and that of their coach, Micky Stewart, were already being widely dissected. After a tour on which no new reputations were made save for bad ones, and where certain existing reputations took a fearful hammering, England's cricket was back in the cul-de-sac it encountered during the Ashes series of 1989. Then, it was the captain who was made accountable. This time, the head-hunters must look elsewhere.

MEN OF THE SERIES

IN A FIVE-MATCH Test series, the most valuable players are those who perform consistently in different conditions and situations and whose efforts noticeably affect the results. Bruce Reid was the best bowler on either side and David Boon the best batsman. No arguments there. Graham Gooch had enough worries with injury and the captaincy, so his efforts with the bat were even more noteworthy. He was the only Englishman to average more than 50. David Gower was the only player to score two centuries but he was too inconsistent. Ian Healy took twenty-four very good catches and played several important innings. Greg Matthews was equally effective, bowling better than his figures suggest and averaging 70.60 with the bat. The efforts of these two highlighted the decisive fact that Australia had the depth to handle pressure situations while England invariably crumbled. Devon Malcolm and Craig McDermott had their moments, but did not do enough to move ahead of Reid, Boon, Gooch, Healy and Matthews.

David Boon

Men of the series

Boon
Matthews
Reid
Healy
Gooch

David Boon typified the strengths of the Australian team in the 1990-91 Ashes series. His reliability under pressure was highly valued and, despite patchy form early in the season, Boon's place was never in jeopardy.

Still, when he walked out to bat late on the fourth day of the second Test with the score on 2-10, he was under more than usual pressure. On the final day of a match dominated by bowlers, a nervous Australia needed 196 to win. After surviving a close leg-before appeal from Devon Malcolm during the tense opening overs, Boon drew on his deep reserves of character to move steadily into his most authoritative form and was undefeated on 94 at the end of the day's play. Boon made a brilliant 97 in Sydney, followed by 49 and 121 in Adelaide and an impressive top score of 64 in Perth against fine fast bowling from Malcolm and Small.

On a range of wickets, Boon was easily his team's most consistent batsman. Without him, Australia's occasional batting lapses might have proved far more costly.

Shot, Boon: The series started slowly for Australia's number three, David Boon, but finished in a blaze of glory. He was leading run-scorer of the series with 530 runs at 75.71.

Underestimated: The 1990-91 Ashes series was a major comeback for Greg Matthews. Matthews is often considered an eccentric first, dedicated cricketer second. Wrong. His dedication to the job saw him back as a front-line spinner, and his magnificent lower-order batting saved Australia several times.

Contented exhaustion: As he contemplates another successful day on the field, the look on Bruce Reid's face says it all. Reid was the dominant bowler of the series – a successful comeback this time after five back operations in the previous two years.

Greg Matthews

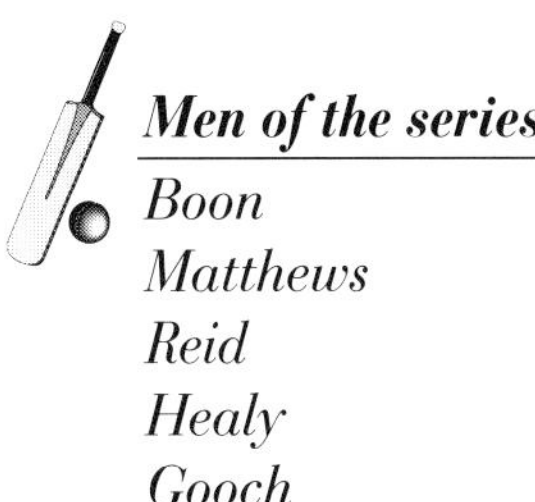

This summer Greg Matthews returned to the Australian team with the firm support of Allan Border. Unlike some critics who consider Matthews's eccentricity a product of selfishness rather than enthusiasm, the Australian captain knew that Matthews had the ability to perform well under pressure.

As a bowler, Matthews did not enjoy much luck in the Ashes series and took only seven wickets. Still, his first wicket was important. In England's first innings in Brisbane, he had Allan Lamb caught, breaking a promising partnership with David Gower and starting the first of England's many collapses.

In Melbourne, with Terry Alderman and Merv Hughes not fully fit, Matthews bowled in tandem with Bruce Reid on the dramatic fourth day when England lost 6-3 in twelve tension-packed overs. In Sydney he took 1-145 off 58 overs, had two catches dropped and for the most part bowled as well as Craig McDermott did in Perth when he took 8-97. Matthews also made a brilliant 128 in the Sydney Test which helped Australia to 518, a total which eventually prevented England from forcing a win.

Throughout the series, the major difference between the teams was that Australia had the will and the depth to recover from setbacks; England did not. On most occasions Greg Matthews played a leading role in those recoveries.

Bruce Reid

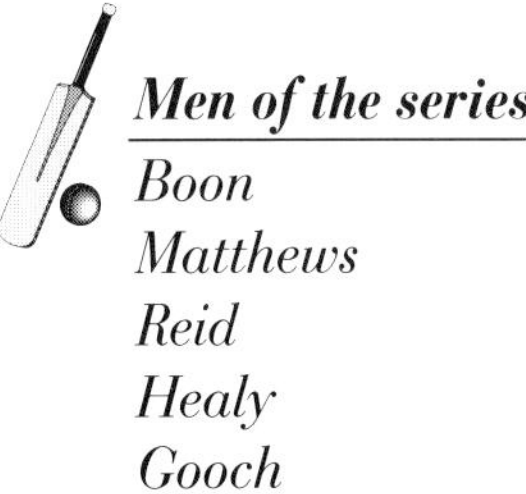

Bruce Reid was the most decisive player of the 1990-91 Ashes series. After five back operations in two years, he had seemed lost forever. But, following excellent early form in his comeback season, Reid was selected for the first Test in Brisbane. He took only five wickets in that match, but in one ball he signalled what was to come. A perfect late-swinging yorker not only shattered Robin Smith's stumps but seriously damaged the morale of an England batting line-up that already had enough to worry about with Terry Alderman.

In the second Test, Reid was brilliant – his 13 for 148 being the second best figures by an Australian since the Second World War. A calloused heel caused him trouble in the next two Tests and finally forced him out of the fifth but, whenever he bowled, Reid was always Australia's most dangerous bowler. His height produced bounce, his angle from left-arm over produced many outside edges and his impeccable control frayed at the jangled nerves of England's helpless batsmen.

Ian Healy

Men of the series
Boon
Matthews
Reid
Healy
Gooch

Like centre-halfs in efficient soccer teams, wicket-keepers usually just finish off the good work of others. In the past, that assessment would have described Ian Healy's performance in the Australian cricket team. But this summer he played a leading role.

After a hesitant start to his Test career in late 1988, Healy began to look far more assured in 1990-91. He took twenty-four catches in the series and, diving for chances that he once would have let pass, began to bring to his keeping the adventurousness that invariably informs his batting.

Healy averaged only 25 with the bat, but on two occasions made valuable contributions when Australia was in trouble. As nightwatchman in Sydney in a tense second-innings battle to deny England an unlikely victory, Healy top-scored with 69, his best total in Test cricket. In Perth he came in when Australia was 6-168 and made 42 off 52 balls. Both times Healy played with an intelligence and a determination that England's middle-to-lower-order batsmen never produced. This proved to be a significant difference between the teams and, in contributing to it, Healy played an important role in Australia's success.

Graham Gooch

Men of the series
Boon
Matthews
Reid
Healy
Gooch

That Graham Gooch left Australia certain to retain the England captaincy and as the only England batsman whose reputation had been enhanced during four disastrous months says much about his character and ability. It was a remarkable achievement, especially given that he missed four weeks of cricket, including the first Test, with a hand injury.

As an individual, Gooch's lowest moment must have been in the first innings of the second Test, his first of the series, when he padded up to Terry Alderman and was out leg-before for 20. In 1989 Alderman so destroyed Gooch that he stood down from the fifth Test. Was history repeating itself? Could Gooch recover his own morale as well as regroup a disintegrating team?

A leader by example, Gooch's next five innings were 58, 59, 54, 87 and 117. His 54 off 42 balls in the second innings in Sydney was a significant gesture. England needed 254 to win off a likely twenty-eight overs, a virtually impossible task, but Gooch batted with great purpose and power. There was a grandeur about his presence at the crease that Australians had only heard of before.

Gooch was the only England batsman to average over 50 for the series and he continually rose above the mediocrity that surrounded him.

Howzat! Ian Healy spent much of the summer off the ground, appealing – sometimes successfully, often unnecessarily. But his efforts behind the stumps were more than workmanlike and his courageous batting was yet another indicator of Australia's all-round domination of the series.

Shining light: 'Graham Gooch versus Australia' may well have been a better title for the series. Gooch was a superb leader: gutsy, aggressive and successful. Despite his personal achievements he will look back on the 1990-91 series with disappointment, due to his team's disastrous performance.

Here we go again: David Gower has a lovely start to his fourth Ashes tour of Australia. A poster-carrying fan met the England team at Perth airport, and made the late TV news with her hero.

What chance England? Cricket manager Micky Stewart ponders the job ahead during a break in practice on the first day of the tour.

Perth, Adelaide, Hobart

GETTING READY

19 OCTOBER – 22 NOVEMBER 1990

The Englishmen could not be as bad as in 1989... could they?

FROM England's point of view the tour started well enough. A sizeable crowd of expatriates, carrying Union Jacks and hand-written posters, welcomed the side at Perth airport late on a Friday night: 19 October. The touring party's three heavies – team manager Peter Lush, cricket manager Micky Stewart and captain Graham Gooch – fielded predictable questions from the welcoming press with predictable answers. Gooch came closest to providing good copy: 'We are not here for the holiday; we are not here for the beer; we are here to play cricket.' Thanks Graham.

The next few days were spent practising at the WACA (Western Australian Cricket Association) ground, with its superb facilities. It was the same sort of perfect weather that had greeted Allan Border's team when it landed at Heathrow at the beginning of May 1989. An omen of good things to come for the tourists?

England started its tour in Perth because Micky Stewart knew the weather would be stable and the practice pitches the fastest and bounciest in Australia. And things went according to Stewart's plan until the fourth full day of the tour.

The team had gone for a centre-wicket practice game at the Melvista Oval in Perth's northern suburbs. Gooch, only just recovered from a broken finger received late in the English season, was bowling to Robin Smith. The powerful, South-African-born batsman launched into one of his thunderous straight drives. Instinctively, Gooch thrust out his right hand to the chance – and the third finger was cut to the bone. The Perth idyll was over.

They say disasters come in threes: first came Gooch's broken thumb in the West Indies, then the broken finger in a county game, now... the horrified look on Micky Stewart's face as Gooch was helped off the practice area was confirmation of his importance to England's Ashes campaign. But the local doctor decided against stitching the wound. Perhaps it was not as bad as it looked.

Next day, Gooch stood down from a match against the Western Australian President's XI at picturesque Lilac Hill, missing a chance to

Oh no, skipper: Graham Gooch was to miss the first four weeks of the tour after injuring his hand at practice.

Remember me? The 41-year-old Dennis Lillee was back in action for the Western Australian President's XI. The old venom was still there, although the express pace was gone. Lillee, who took 167 wickets at 21.00 in 29 Tests against England, last played for Australia in 1984.

confront England's old foe, the 41-year-old Dennis Lillee, who'd agreed to roll a few down. But three days later, England's captain played in a two-day game against Western Australia Country, at Geraldton, some three hundred kilometres north of Perth on the far west coast of the continent. Gooch survived the wilds of Geraldton and played in a one-day match, then in the tour's first four-day game against a strong Western Australian team. He described his footwork as 'feet in concrete' but at least he was playing. It seemed the injury was a minor setback. England avoided defeat by Western Australia by only one wicket, thanks to Robin Smith and Allan Lamb. The tourists headed east for Adelaide chastened and vowing to lift a cog or two.

But further disaster awaited. On the second morning of the match against South Australia, Gooch failed to take the field. That evening, a morose team manager, Peter Lush, told the press that Gooch's finger had become swollen and sore at the nets before play and that he had been admitted to a private hospital.

Worse news came the next day when it was revealed that Gooch had undergone surgery on the now poisoned finger. After three weeks in Australia, England faced the certain prospect of being without its captain for the first Test in Brisbane. As Gooch said, while his poisoned finger recovered from surgery: 'It's ironic that after years without any problems I've had three hand injuries in the space of eight months. And each injury has come at a critical time.'

A man of few words and fewer expressive gestures, Gooch's competitiveness and professionalism had rubbed off on a team that had been drifting aimlessly. He had been a major factor in England's recovery from its 4-0 thrashing by Border's Australians in 1989.

England's top-order batting already looked vulnerable, with openers Mike Atherton and Wayne Larkins, and David Gower at number three, all struggling for runs. Without Gooch, who during the 1990 English summer had made an awesome 1058 runs in the six Tests against New Zealand and India, there was a huge hole to fill and no one who looked remotely capable of filling it. Gooch had dominated England's batting in its best home Test series for many years, with an average of 96.18 and a remarkable top score of 333. His leadership was an unexpected bonus.

Despite concern about his leadership qualities, Allan Lamb took over the captaincy. In its next game, as if to confirm doubts about the team without Gooch, England lost to South Australia, widely regarded as the weakest team in the Sheffield Shield.

While Gooch stayed in hospital in Adelaide, his team went south to Hobart for a tough four-day match against an Australian XI containing the best of the country's up-and-coming players. England's fortunes looked up in Hobart, thanks largely to Lamb and fast bowler Devon Malcolm. After yet another worrying top-order collapse, with Atherton, Larkins and Gower all out for a total of 9 on the first morning, Lamb thrashed the young Australians for a superb 154. This was the first first-class hundred of the tour by an England player. Smith made 71 and Alec Stewart an impressive 95.

Lamb was responding to the leadership challenge in the way he knew best. In the second innings he thrashed a hundred in a session on the last morning of the game, after the top three had gone for only 19. England looked like it had replaced one inspirational leader with another.

The other good news for England was Malcolm's brilliant 7-74 in the Australians' first innings. After three weeks of wayward bowling, the man England was relying on so heavily for early wickets had found form.

The Englishmen seemed to feel more at home in cold and showery Hobart and they finally had the better of a match, although it was a draw. But even then, the good form of Lamb, Stewart, Smith and Malcolm was countered by runs in both innings from David Boon, Australia's number three, and wickets from Queensland's Craig McDermott.

It was only when Australians remembered how poorly Mike Gatting's 1986-87 England team had begun its tour and how easily it had eventually won the Test series that their optimism about the coming summer was tempered. Otherwise the omens looked better than ever for Australia.

Bruce Reid, returning after serious surgery on his back, offered the Australian selectors a snippet of what might be. In the Western Australian Invitation XI's one-day game against England in Perth, he took 1-15 off ten impressive overs. When he not only took that same form into Western Australia's four-day match against the tourists, but hit Lamb's elbow with

IN PROFILE

Allan Lamb

Born: 20.6.54

Tests: 70. Debut v. India, Lord's, 1982.

Highest score: 139 v. India, Lord's, 1990.

Nickname: Legga or Lambie.

Favourite moment: Our win against the West Indies in Jamaica in 1990.

Horror moment: That's not easy to answer. I suppose being left out of the England side after playing quite a few Test matches.

Greatest influence: While I was at school in South Africa it was my dad, Mickie, and after I left school, Hilton Ackerman.

Superstitions: Sometimes if I'm scoring runs I try to wear the same shirt all the time.

Favourite shot: The two shots that look nice are the hook and the cover drive. A genuine cover drive is hard to beat.

How do you overcome nerves? I always have butterflies. You just have to try to relax, to tell yourself it's not the end of the world, that if you fail today you won't be dead.

Coaching tip: Number 1: watch the ball. Number 2: stand still and play in the V between mid-off and mid-on.

IN PROFILE

Steve Waugh

Born: 2.6.65

Tests: 42. Debut v. India, Melbourne, 1985-86.

Best figures: 177 not out v. England, Headingley, 1989. 5-69 v. England, Perth, 1986-87.

Nickname: Tugga.

Favourite moment: Winning the World Cup final, and my first Test century at Headingley in 1989.

Horror moment: I suppose getting dropped from the Test side this summer.

Greatest influence: Going to watch Test matches as a kid and watching games on television. Over the past few years Bob Simpson has been a great help.

Superstitions: When you are going well you look for little things. In England in 1989 I didn't shave during a game but I've stopped that. I put my left pad on first but that's more a habit.

Favourite shot/delivery: My favourite shot has to be the back-foot cover drive. My favourite delivery is probably the out-swinger when it works. I enjoy bowling a good slower ball too.

How do you overcome nerves? That's a tough question. Bradman said he didn't feel nervous because he was always confident of success. But most players get nervous. I like to sit by myself before I go in to bat and just watch the game quietly.

Coaching tip: Stick to your natural game.

a quick one which lifted nastily off a length, one of Australia's best bowlers was back on the books.

At the other end of the country, Craig McDermott was rampaging through Sheffield Shield batting line-ups. The raw teenager, who showed so much promise when he made his Test debut against the West Indies in 1984-85, had been on the outer for the past few years. Too much too soon, it seemed. Now he was back, as fit as the iron-men he trained with during what passes for winter in Queensland, off a shorter run and bowling outswingers at pace.

With Chris Matthews, Reid's Western Australian team-mate, also taking wickets with his mystifying mixture of rubbish and unplayable deliveries, Australia's pace bowling depth was formidable. Terry Alderman, Merv Hughes and Carl Rackemann would be there again and Geoff Lawson was still bowling well.

Of the Test batsmen, Geoff Marsh had been in great touch, including 151 for Western Australia against England. Australia's captain, Allan Border, had been in good form, posting a run of 60s and 70s without reaching the three-figure mark that eludes him so often these days. Before the summer, Border said publicly that he felt as keen as ever. The depth of young talent in Australian cricket and the form of his Test side was keeping him going.

Steve Waugh was also making decent scores and offering the promise of better things to come. His twin brother, Mark, and Tom Moody were carrying on from where they left off in county cricket a month or so before.

Mark Taylor began slowly in the domestic one-day series before making a quiet little 183 in his first first-class innings for New South Wales. Soon after, he fractured a finger in a match in rural Wagga Wagga, missed the next Shield game and was in doubt for the first Test. Were the fates evening up for Gooch's injury?

Of the other batsmen, Dean Jones and David Boon had been struggling. Boon eventually came good in Hobart but, even so, the general feeling in Australia was that these Test players were now good enough to lift when they had to. Australia's cricketers had learned how to win and the public had grown to expect it.

Patriotic over-confidence or sound cricket judgement? The Englishmen could not be as bad as in 1989... could they? Only time would tell. But it was still doubtful whether England had the ability and nerve to regain the Ashes against such a talented and confident Australian team.

The Ashes 1986-90

SINCE England's victorious tour of Australia for the 1986-87 Test series, each team has alternately showed promise and fallen into disarray.

In the early weeks of the 1986-87 Australian summer, England's form was dismal. But the first Test in Brisbane saw the inexperienced Australians waste the advantage of winning the toss. They bowled poorly on the first day and Ian Botham drew on reserves of pride, ability and experience to make a match-winning 138. Australia never recovered and England won the Ashes 2-1. Australia's only victory came on the turning Sydney wicket.

For the 1990-91 tour, only Allan Lamb, David Gower, Phil DeFreitas and Gladstone Small survived from Mike Gatting's winning 1986-87 side. Age, loss of form, disillusionment caused by poor selections over several years, dalliances with barmaids and defections to South Africa combined to change England's team greatly from the previously victorious tourists.

And over those four years, as England sank further and further into the pits, Australia gradually lifted. Allan Border provided stoic leadership, with support from Geoff Lawson, Terry Alderman and other senior players. David Boon, Dean Jones and Steve Waugh began to justify the faith that had been invested in them. Fortunes really began to change for Australia when it beat Gatting's team in the final of the World Cup at Eden Gardens, Calcutta, in 1987. Then the side did reasonably well against New Zealand at home and Pakistan away. Progress was slow but encouraging.

Then came the West Indies tour of Australia in 1988-89. Border's team

ENGLAND IN AUSTRALIA 1986-87

England captain: Mike Gatting – Australia captain: Allan Border

FIRST TEST
Brisbane, 14–19 November
England: 456 (IT Botham 138, CWJ Athey 76, MW Gatting 61, DI Gower 51), 3-77
Australia: 248 (GR Marsh 56, GRJ Matthews 56*. GR Dilley 5-68), 282 (GR Marsh 110. JE Emburey 5-80)
England won by 7 wickets

SECOND TEST
Perth, 28 November–3 December
England: 8d-592 (BC Broad 162, DI Gower 136, CJ Richards 133, CWJ Athey 96. BA Reid 4-115), 8d-199 (MW Gatting 70. SR Waugh 5-69)
Australia: 401 (AR Border 125, SR Waugh 71. GR Dilley 4-79), 4-197 (DM Jones 69)
Match drawn

THIRD TEST
Adelaide, 12–16 December
Australia: 5d-514 (DC Boon 103, DM Jones 93, SR Waugh 79*, GRJ Matthews 73*, AR Border 70), 3d-201 (AR Border 100*)
England: 455 (BC Broad 116, MW Gatting 100, CWJ Athey 55. BA Reid 4-64, PR Sleep 4-132), 2-39
Match drawn

FOURTH TEST
Melbourne, 26–28 December
Australia: 141 (DM Jones 59. GC Small 5-48, IT Botham 5-41), 194 (GR Marsh 60. PH Edmonds 3-45)
England: 349 (BC Broad 112. BA Reid 4-78, CJ McDermott 4-83)
England won by an innings and 14 runs

FIFTH TEST
Sydney, 10–15 January
Australia: 343 (DM Jones 184*. GC Small 5-75), 251 (SR Waugh 73. JE Emburey 7-78)
England: 275 (DI Gower 72, JE Emburey 69. PL Taylor 6-78), 264 (MW Gatting 96. PR Sleep 5-72)
Australia won by 55 runs

But the third Test, in Melbourne, was the turning point. In a vicious game, in which the West Indies bowled with frightening speed, the Australians lost but showed great courage in defeat. The team character was hardened in this fierce match and results improved dramatically. The Australians won the next match, in Sydney, then drew well in Adelaide. They arrived in London for the 1989 Ashes series a united, quietly confident side.

For England, the summer of 1989 was a tale of woe. Ted Dexter had taken over the selecting and running of English cricket and great things were expected. England had used thirty-one players in the previous season against the touring West Indians and was thrashed. Despite Dexter's assurances of stability, England went on to use twenty-nine players against Australia. The reason was an equal mixture of a bad run of injuries, poor individual performances and defections to Gatting's sad and eventually aborted rebel tour of South Africa.

Australia regained the Ashes convincingly, winning the series 4-0, with two matches drawn.

The highlight of 1989 for England was the emergence of pace bowler Angus Fraser, batsman Robin Smith and wicket-keeper Jack Russell. All looked Test players from the start.

After that series, England regrouped impressively. Graham Gooch, replacing Gower as captain, inspired his team on its tour of the Caribbean in March and April 1990. England led the West Indies 1-0 after two Test matches but, without Gooch, whose thumb was broken in the third

The old guard: England's chairman of selectors Ted Dexter and a bemused David Gower faced the press after yet another England failure during Australia's 1989 triumphant Ashes tour.

match, lost the series 2-1. Still, some pride had been restored. Back home, much the same team won three-match Tests against New Zealand and India. Not great teams, but victories nonetheless.

The England team arriving in Australia in October 1990 combined relatively untried youth: Chris Lewis, Devon Malcolm, Phil Tufnell and Martin Bicknell; with established youth: Mike Atherton and Angus Fraser; and an older brigade of experienced campaigners: Gooch, Gower, Lamb, Small and Hemmings. And blended with this, a renewed emphasis on fitness, technique and long-term planning.

Australia consolidated steadily in 1989-90, against New Zealand, Sri Lanka and Pakistan. Mark Taylor and Dean Jones confirmed their reputations as two of the best batsmen in the world, but the bowlers were occasionally found wanting. However, there seemed to be a depth of talent there that had been missing for many years. Early in the 1990 summer season, only Jones struggled for runs. Most importantly, the tall left-arm paceman, Bruce Reid, bowled beautifully after a year's recovery from serious back surgery. His inclusion in the first Test team was perhaps the best news for Australian cricket since Taylor's plundering of England in 1989.

England and Australia are not the two best cricket teams in the world – as they were up to the 1960s, before the emergence of the West Indies. But as the teams gathered, the 1990-91 Ashes series promised to be more evenly contested and better than 1989's one-sided affair.

Warming up: Stretching exercises on the morning of the first Test, Headingley, 1989.

AUSTRALIA IN ENGLAND 1989

Australia captain: Allan Border – England captain: David Gower

FIRST TEST
Headingley, 8–13 June
Australia: 7d-601 (SR Waugh 177*, MA Taylor 136, DM Jones 79, MG Hughes 71, AR Border 66), 3d-230 (MA Taylor 60, AR Border 60)
England: 430 (AJ Lamb 125, KJ Barnett 80, RA Smith 66. TM Alderman 5-107), 191 (GA Gooch 68. TM Alderman 5-44)
Australia won by 210 runs

SECOND TEST
Lord's, 22–27 June
England: 286 (RC Russell 64*, GA Gooch 60, DI Gower 57. MG Hughes 4-71), 359 (DI Gower 106, RA Smith 96. TM Alderman 6 128)
Australia: 528 (SR Waugh 152*, DC Boon 94, GF Lawson 74, MA Taylor 64. JE Emburey 4-88), 4-119 (DC Boon 58*)
Australia won by 6 wickets

THIRD TEST
Edgbaston, 6–11 July
Australia: 424 (DM Jones 157. ARC Fraser 4-62), 2-158 (MA Taylor 51)
England: 242 (IT Botham 46, RC Russell 42, TS Curtis 41)
Match drawn

FOURTH TEST
Old Trafford, 27 July–1 August
England: 260 (RA Smith 143. GF Lawson 6-72), 264 (RC Russell 128*, JE Emburey 64. TM Alderman 5-66)
Australia: 447 (SR Waugh 92, MA Taylor 85, AR Border 80, DM Jones 69), 1-81
Australia won by 9 wickets

FIFTH TEST
Trent Bridge, 10–14 August
Australia: 6d-602 (MA Taylor 219, GR Marsh 138, DC Boon 73, AR Border 65)
England: 255 (RA Smith 101. TM Alderman 5-69), 167 (MA Atherton 47. SR Waugh 3-46)
Australia won by an innings and 180 runs

SIXTH TEST
The Oval, 24–29 August
Australia: 468 (DM Jones 122, AR Border 76, MA Taylor 71. DR Pringle 4-70), 4-219 (AR Border 51*, DM Jones 50)
England: 285 (DI Gower 79, GC Small 59. TM Alderman 5-66), 5-143 (RA Smith 77)
Match drawn

Keeping cool: England's fast-bowling hope, Devon Malcolm, enjoying centre-wicket practice in Perth, during the first week of the tour.

Take it easy, Devon, take it easy

DURING the first month of the Ashes tour no player had more eyes watching him than fast bowler Devon Malcolm. Quite obviously, England was trying hard to turn the inexperienced Jamaican-born quick into a fully-fledged Test bowler.

During net sessions, if cricket manager Micky Stewart was not watching every move Malcolm made, one of the other fast bowlers was. Every time Malcolm managed to keep his head upright and his feet in the correct positions, calls of encouragement came from all directions. 'Well bowled Devvie. That's it, Devvie.'

Off the field, Malcolm moves slowly, as if he is permanently at the end of a long, hard day's work under a hot sun. He is a true West Indian.

At a centre-wicket practice in Perth, Malcolm began by sitting under the shade of some trees doing a television interview while his colleagues toiled in the sun.

'Ey, Devon, what you doin' out there?' called the conscientious and slightly mischievous Angus Fraser. 'You gonna bowl at some stage or what?'

When Malcolm does bowl, things happen. That same week he nearly took Robin Smith's head off with two consecutive bouncers that flew off the fast WACA practice wickets.

Malcolm is a one-off in the touring England team. He lacks the self-conscious finesse of most England cricketers. For him, technique is a necessary evil, not an end in itself. He is raw but potentially valuable and so is treated differently; occasionally criticised but most often encouraged, even when he is only doing what he should.

And later: Devon Malcolm finds another way to avoid the heat of the sun, and the toil of practice.

Twice in the first fortnight in Perth, Stewart had to berate Malcolm publicly for slovenliness. Stewart played down the incidents, explaining: 'Devon is the sort of bloke who takes four and a half hours to put on his shoes.'

Could this comparative slackness be evidence of immaturity, of a weakness of temperament?

Malcolm is as unpredictable as Fraser is constant. He sprays the ball all over the place like a bloodthirsty drunk firing a machine gun. If one shot hits the bull's eye, all sorts of damage is done – as shown by his forty-two wickets from only eleven Tests. But if Malcolm wastes too many shots, the Australians could take a heavy toll.

Even before England left Old Blighty, Australian batsmen heard that one plan was for Malcolm to take them on. Jones, Taylor and Waugh – the three who caused most damage in 1989 – would be tested with plenty of short stuff. Since Malcolm would never become a swing bowler, such a tactic made sense. With the classy and reliable Fraser at the other end applying genuine Test-match pressure, Malcolm could be devastating. But there was always the risk that if he gave the Australians width they would surely go for their shots, testing Malcolm's temperament and countering England's major hope.

After taking 4-223 in the first two first-class matches, Malcolm suddenly got it right in Hobart. His 7-74 in the Australian XI's first innings showed how dangerous he could be.

Devon Malcolm and Angus Fraser versus the Australians. It was certainly going to be exciting; it could also be decisive.

Bruce Reid: third time lucky

WHEN BRUCE REID found some extra pace and bounce and lifted a ball painfully into Allan Lamb's defending elbow in the four-day game against England early in the season, the Englishmen saw something they did not need to see. Reid's new chest-on action, remodelled to avoid further damage to his long and fragile spine, had not lessened his ability to swing the ball back in to the right-hander, a deadly delivery, or lift it sharply as it veered across the batsman towards the slips, a constant test of the batsmen's reflexes.

Reid had not played for Australia since his back caved in on the 1988 tour of Pakistan. Since then he had undergone five operations and two aborted comebacks. The final operation inserted a five-centimetre metal plate in his lower spine.

Until this Test, most Australian cricket followers had written Reid off: a world-class bowler broken by a thin, vulnerable body. But the Australian selectors were tempted by his early form..

Reid's selection for the first Test was an aggressive gamble. But, as the selectors knew, he could be rested from some of the one-day series between the first and second Tests. Too much strain too early on that reconstructed back could cause the breakdown everyone feared.

Reid is a casual character, but even he realised the dangers of taking his comeback too lightly. He had declined an offer to play in Western Australia's final games the season before. During the winter he swam kilometre after kilometre and regularly went through a series of exercises designed to strengthen and prepare his back for a return to first-class cricket. During the Ashes series there was no let-up to this regime. Reid explained: 'Every day I have to do extra crunches (abbreviated sit-ups) and push-ups. And I try to swim each day. The thing is I can't sit back and take a day off even if I'm feeling well. You can get away with that if you have no injury problems, but I can't afford to slacken off at all.'

'Then after each day's play I have to do warm-down exercises. They help to alleviate the muscle stiffness in that area of the back which is my only problem now. Basically, it's more psychological than anything. If you know you're doing the right thing, you feel better. As for exercise outside cricket, it's a matter of being sensible. My doctor advised me to play golf as it would loosen me up. But I only play after a match, never before.'

Reid was an enormous boost to the Australian attack. It seemed that, as long as his body held up, he would add significantly to Australia's bowling strength that, even without him, had destroyed England's batting in 1989.

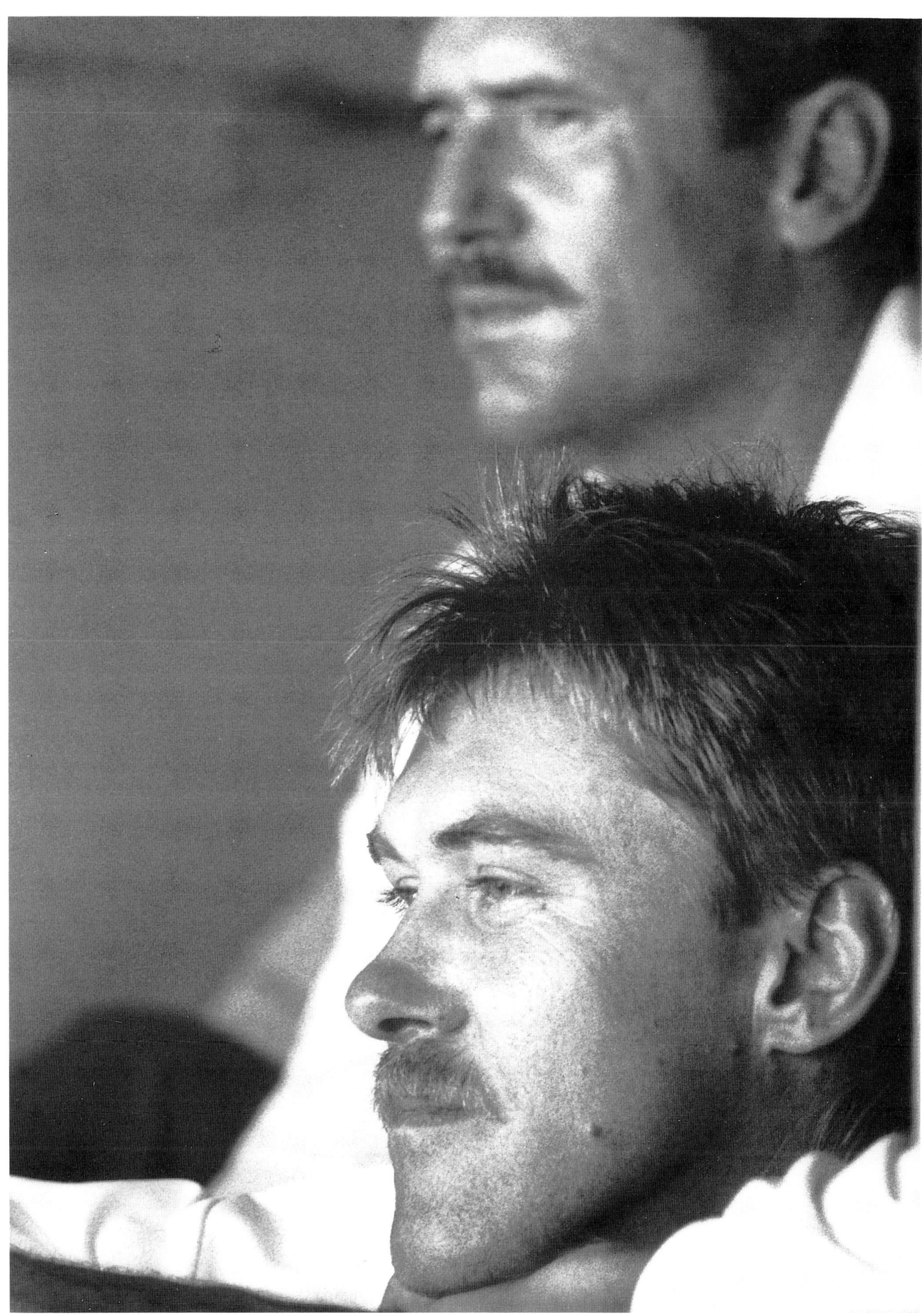

Back in business: Bruce Reid's selection for the first Test was just reward for a marvellous comeback from a serious injury. His pace, accuracy and left-hander's angle completed a potent fast-bowling attack for skipper Allan Border.

Graham Gooch: a sorry sight

The English view

Alan Lee looks behind the public face of the England captain.

THERE was something symbolic about the sight. Graham Gooch, bush hat perched atop those familiar lugubrious, stubbled features, a flesh-coloured scaffolding over his right hand, plodded across the lobby of Brisbane's Hilton Hotel, alone and detached. England, his England, must once again muddle through without him, and nobody could be confident it was capable of it.

Consumed by the work ethic, conditioned into positive thinking, it is doubtful whether the England party permitted any melancholy thoughts over such things as the worst conceivable pre-series prognosis. If they had, no one would have looked further than the loss of Gooch. Inspirational as captain, indispensable as a batsman, Gooch's stock had not stopped climbing throughout 1990. Launching an already intimidating Ashes campaign without him would be immeasurably more difficult; poignantly, it was Gooch himself who had to convince his colleagues they could do it.

For the worst part of a fortnight, Gooch was imprisoned in an Adelaide hospital. Private room, to be sure. Television and telephone to hand and celebrity visitors, Eric Clapton among them, flocking to his bedside. Outstanding nurses, too, so Gooch said. But a touch of pampering and an overdose of relaxation could be no cure for frustration when your greatest wish was to take home the Ashes and the show was about to start without you.

Gooch has never been one to make a public showing of his innermost thoughts. Quite the opposite. His natural hangdog expression and his determinedly private personality has had him cast as miserable, solitary and uncommunicative. All, as it happens, hogwash, but the labels stuck and convinced the vast majority that, when the leadership of the England cricket team became an issue once more, the candidature of G.A. Gooch could be dismissed as entirely unsuitable. Even those who had known him longest and counted themselves among his supporters were sceptical.

In the Caribbean, early in 1990, Gooch was a revelation to us all. He took apparently ordinary players, fresh from an extraordinary Ashes débâcle, and made them a unit which thoroughly shook up the West Indies. He has the gift, possessed by few and defined by virtually no one, of relating to individuals within a team game, treating them all differently and yet targeting each of them in the same ultimate direction. He does it, strikingly, without visible change in his character. Outwardly, he remains hangdog and humdrum and, on the quiet, I think he has begun to enjoy the erroneous image.

When Gooch was injured on the cataclysmic final day of the Trinidad Test in March, a game which England won everywhere but at the finishing tape, the captaincy of the side passed to Allan Lamb. The next two Tests were lost, one valiantly, the second sacrificially, and although this was an awesome time to be put in the dock, Lamb suffered by comparison. He is a natural number two, an irrepressible cheerleader of a man who plays his cricket with unquenchable spirit and energy and expects others to do just the same. Tactically, there has never been the quiet air of command about him which is so impressive in Gooch. Now, with history repeating itself all too rapidly, Lamb was once more in charge, Gooch once more a wounded bystander.

Gooch was not sure to be fit for the second Test, despite the fact that the Australian Cricket Board, in its baffling wisdom, had scheduled a gap of a month between games. But in Brisbane, where the curator promised a 'result pitch' and where England's strength – the seam bowling of Angus Fraser and Gladstone Small – may have given them their best chance of a critical early lead, he could do no more than advise. It was not encouraging.

Watchers: England skipper Graham Gooch and Australian coach Bob Simpson talk shop before the first Test.

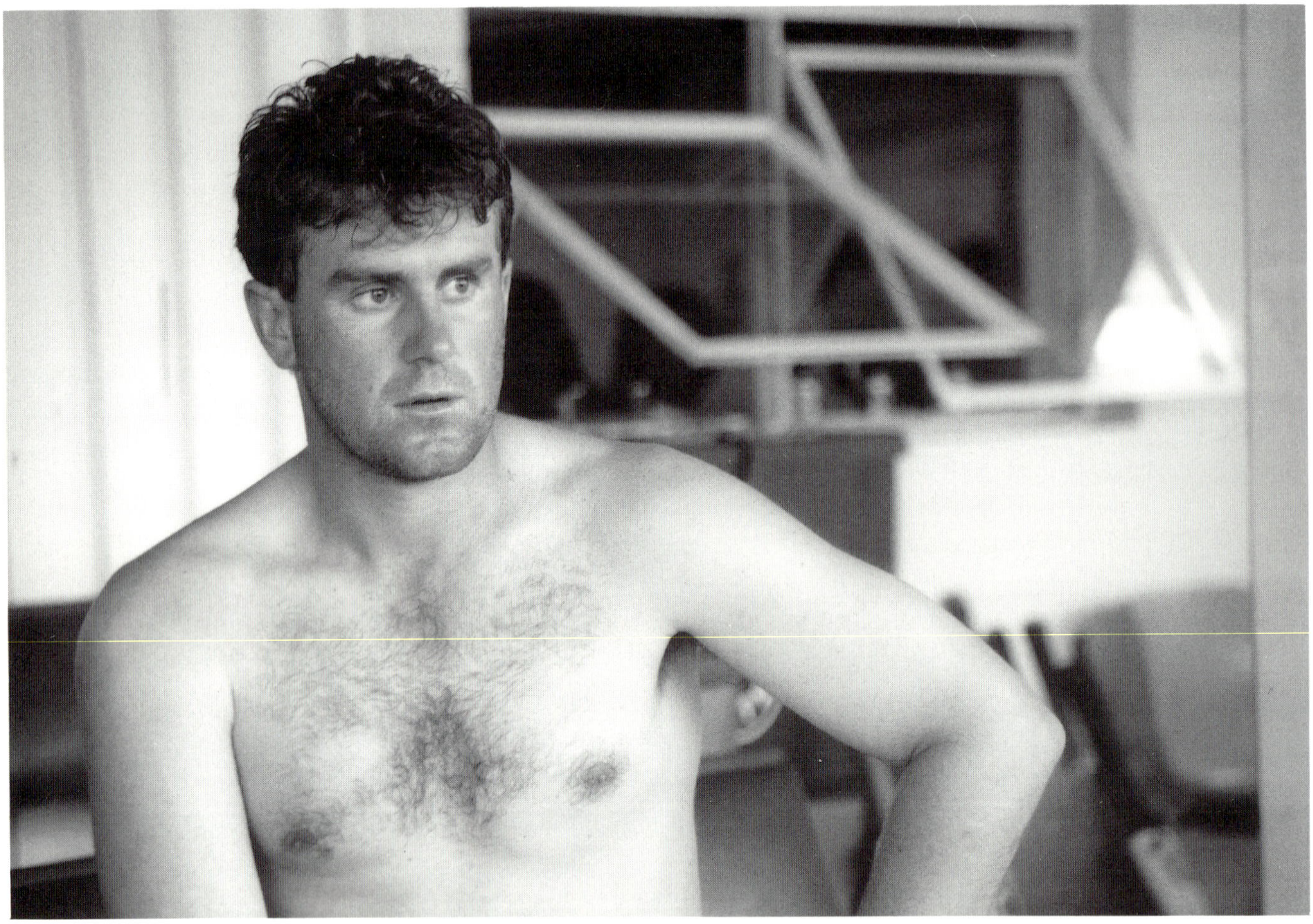

Determined: Mark Taylor started the summer with a Bradmanesque batting average, but it didn't help him sleep before leaving for Brisbane and the battles ahead.

So much hinges on the first Test

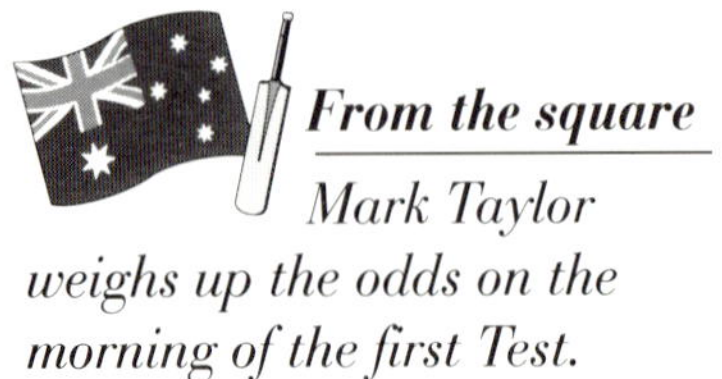

From the square

Mark Taylor weighs up the odds on the morning of the first Test.

"WHEN I broke my finger in the game at Wagga two weeks before the first Test, I was told it would have to be pinned and I'd be out for a month. Fortunately the specialist I saw disagreed. He said if I missed the coming Sheffield Shield game in Melbourne I'd be able to bat in the Test with no problems. And he was right. If I get a knock on the finger while fielding it does hurt, but it doesn't worry me at all when I'm batting.

At least I'm hitting them all right. I started this season as I always do: a hundred in the first club game, then a short slump and finally a big score. My opening first-class knock was 183. I haven't had a hit since then but at least I've had one long stretch in the middle.

People have been saying I must be feeling the pressure to perform after such a good series against England in 1989, but I don't see it that way. I feel I've already done well against them. They know I'm a good player. I'm happy with my Test career. I'm not getting complacent but I don't think there's any extra pressure, especially because we have such a strong batting line-up. The way I'm thinking is if I don't get them someone else will.

That is why it was good to see Boonie make runs against England in Hobart. It was a good sign for all of us, because Devon obviously bowled well down there but Boonie made runs against him. Devon's not Superman.

I am not sure what to expect from him. He'll be thinking about last time in Nottingham when Swampy (Geoff Marsh) and I put on 329. He bowled pretty well in his first spell, but he tended to bowl a yard too short. And he didn't come back well in later spells. We got a four off him every two overs and I can't see any reason why we won't play him the same way this time. If he's short or wide we'll play our shots.

The pressure is on Devon more than us, especially because England is relying on him so much. If we can be 0-50 or so at lunch, I think we have the batsmen down the order to build a big score.

It was terrific to get back with the team. I couldn't sleep at home on Tuesday night I was so keyed up about going to Brisbane in the morning. I realise this first Test is going to be crucial. At Headingley in 1989 everyone was saying how important the first Test would be, but it seemed like just another big game for me, being only my third Test. It wasn't until after the series that I realised the significance of the win there.

We've had the customary team meeting held on the night before the Test and we've discussed the English players in depth. We'd looked at the wicket after training and talked about batting first should we win the toss. However, there has been a thunderstorm overnight and there's a thick cloud cover. We'll bowl if we win the toss.

So much hinges on the first Test: whoever wins gets away to a quick start. If we can win easily here, I can't see any reason why we can't win 3-0 or 4-0. But England obviously played well in the West Indies and if they play well here they could give us a run for our money. ”

IN PROFILE

Mark Taylor

Born: 27.10.64

Tests: 20. Debut v. West Indies, Sydney, 1988-89.

Highest score: 219 v. England, Trent Bridge, 1989.

Nickname: Tubby or Tails.

Favourite moment: Being on the field at Old Trafford batting with Boonie when we won the Ashes.

Horror moment: It's a good time to ask. Yep, the Adelaide Test match, when I was run out in the second innings (making it twice out that way in two of the three Test matches I've played there).

Greatest influence: My father, Tony. He taught me the basics of the game. And Neil Marks when I stepped up to first-class cricket. I had a bad year the third season and he talked me through.

Superstitions: None. I had a few, like putting my left pad on first, but I've weeded them out in the past couple of years.

Favourite shot: Front-foot cover drive I'd say, and probably the square cut.

How do you overcome nerves? I don't really try to. I don't think they're necessarily a bad thing. Everyone has nerves. Bowlers have nerves about being hit to the boundary all the time and batsmen have nerves about getting out, so I think everyone's feeling the same. But you try not to show them too much.

Coaching tip: Keep it simple. That's all I'd say. Keep it simple and don't think too much about it.

Hands off: Reading The Hunt for Red October *was one way for Graham Gooch to escape the agony of missing the action.*

Brisbane

THE FIRST TEST

23 – 25 NOVEMBER 1990

AS IF TO emphasise the fact that the cricket temperature was about to rise, England left antarctic Hobart for tropical Brisbane to prepare for the first Test. Acting captain Allan Lamb had already complained how few first-class matches England had played before the Test series opened. Landing in steamy Brisbane after Hobart only seemed to emphasise that the crunch was coming, ready or not.

Graham Gooch and Mark Taylor joined their teams two days before the Test match, but with a crucial difference. Taylor was fit to play; Gooch's arm still bandaged and in a sling. He would watch the game from the bench under a newly-acquired Akubra hat, but at least he was there and not recuperating back in England – a move he had considered briefly in hospital in Adelaide.

Although the Australians were favourites, England's improved form in the Hobart game reminded everyone that Test teams tend to coast early in a tour and that their form can change dramatically when the big games start. You only had to look back to the last England tour (1986-87) for the evidence. Early in the piece it was said that Mike Gatting's team could not 'bat, bowl or field'. But how wrong that proved to be. Australia won the toss in the first Test in Brisbane, bowled poorly and eventually lost the game. Then the series.

The question now was whether this England team had the ability, experience and desire to turn things around as Gatting's had done four years earlier. Then, Ian Botham had made a disciplined century in the first Test and forged the way ahead. It seemed there was no one in this England team who remotely approached Botham as a match-winner.

As well, Australia's bowlers were no longer green and wayward. They were not going to waste the new ball and the toss as their predecessors had four years before. Australia had proven itself in 1989 and though England had shown improvement since that 4-0 drubbing, Australia's form was still better and more consistent.

You can often tell a lot about a cricket team by the way it trains and in Brisbane the differences between the teams were very noticeable. The

'I can't recall a Test quite like it,' said the Australian captain.

Captains: Allan Lamb took over from Graham Gooch. For Allan Border it was business as usual.

Batting order: To be a Test player you have to have plenty of time for souvenir signing. Dean Jones contemplates life at the top.

day before the game, England batted and bowled at a local private school then drove to the Gabba for a fielding session. It was a disrupted, disjointed and unimpressive effort. No spark yet.

The Australians did in two hours what England did not quite manage in three. Half the Englishmen were still out having catches when the Australians had enjoyed a competitive, fun-filled practice session, signed the two dozen autograph bats lined up outside the dressing-rooms, showered and left for a free afternoon.

Cricket teams usually play the way they train. England was leaving it dangerously late to lift its game.

As usual on the day before a Test, the wicket was the centre of attention. Dean Jones walked down it and offered his usual confident assessment: 'It will do a bit for the first session or so and then be a belter for two days.' There are no shades of grey in Jones's world.

Steve Waugh followed Jones a few minutes later, tapping the wicket with his bat as he went. 'That's strange,' he said, 'sounds a bit hollow to me. Like an English wicket.' Where Jones sees only black or white, Waugh sees shades of grey. He does not place his trust in things too readily and he was suspicious about this wicket. Given the recent winning record for teams bowling first at the Gabba, the toss would again be important.

England was to play four pace bowlers. There was no speculation about its final eleven. Australia's twelfth man would come from either Greg Matthews, Merv Hughes or Carl Rackemann. Border wanted

See you tomorrow, mate: Robin Smith and Geoff Marsh looking forward to the start of the series.

Matthews. He said, 'In last season's Shield final Matthews was a class above anyone I've faced for a long time, and that's anyone in the world.' So either Hughes or Rackemann would miss out. As ever, the Australian selectors would have to balance current form (Rackemann) with sustained good service (Hughes), but whatever the decision, it was never going to be crucial. Both bowlers could be relied upon.

Unless Border lost the toss and his batsmen suffered on a seaming wicket, it looked like Australia had the form and the ability to win the opening game. And, as recent history showed, whoever won the first Test would probably go on to win the series. Both teams were well aware of that.

Day one

Welcome back, Bruce Reid

NOT ONLY was England's cricket team without its leader for the first Test but, as Brisbane's papers announced on day one, their nation was soon to be without its long-serving Prime Minister, Margaret Thatcher. The Iron Lady had resigned and, although Thatcher's departure might have been bad tidings for some, for that small band of English cricketers in Australia the skipper's absence was the worst imaginable news.

England, with no alternative, chose an all-pace attack. The spinners, Hemmings and Tufnell, had no hope. They had had little bowling, which suggested that the English selectors had made up their minds about their first Test team weeks ahead. Hemmings had been pretty much a full-time tourist, complete with sore back, and you had to wonder about how much he would contribute on the tour. Tufnell had shown promise in his limited time at the crease, but English conservatism acceded to Brisbane's reputation for helping the seamers.

Devon Malcolm was preferred ahead of Martin Bicknell in a move that could be reversed as the summer progressed. There were doubts about Malcolm's true worth right up to the start of play, with some observers believing, not without justification, that Bicknell's slower outswingers would provide the variety otherwise lacking. As well, Bicknell had shown more competitive spark than most of the other bowlers .

On the Australian side, Border, true to his word, went for variety by including the off-spinner Matthews. Hughes, who had probably backed himself in as outright favourite for twelfth man, was preferred to Rackemann. This was typical of Australia's selectors. Rackemann had been looking sharper than Hughes in the lead-up games but Hughes's efforts during the past year earned him the spot. And deservedly so. No one in the Australian team had worked harder.

Under high cloud Border won the toss and sent England in on a green wicket. When, in the third over, Larkins on-drove Alderman for four, a

IN PROFILE

Greg Matthews

Born: 15.12.59

Tests: 26. Debut v. Pakistan, Melbourne, 1983-84.

Best Figures: 130 v. New Zealand, Wellington, 1985-86; 5-103 v. India, Madras, 1968-87.

Nickname: Mo. It used to be Misère but when Imran Khan played for New South Wales he pronounced it Mosère then called me Michale Mo or Moster and the Mo has stuck.

Favourite moment: The tied Test in Madras in 1986. The whole game was magic, especially the last over.

Horror moment: 1-145. That's it.

Greatest influence: Gordon Nolan, my coach out at Ermington in Sydney from the time I was eight years old.

Superstitions: None really.

Favourite shot/delivery: Anything that gets me runs and anything that gets an out.

How do you overcome nerves? I don't know how to. I don't think nerves are a bad thing either. They get the adrenalin going.

Coaching tip: Never give up; you can do anything if you want it badly enough.

stirring shout of 'Shaaart, Ned' burst from the back of the press box. Columnist and former England captain Mike Gatting was getting excited. England's supporters were daring to hope.

Sadly, they would have had more reason to hope had Gatting been padded up to go in next playing that combative, aggressive cricket that was so much admired. Tragically, history and the krugerrand put paid to that.

England's hopes were short-lived. Reid and Matthews, the former returning from a crippling back injury and the latter having overturned opinion about his game and character, made crucial breakthroughs and showed quickly that they would strengthen Australia's attack.

Reid was tentative in the early overs, admitting later that he had been so nervous that sweat had been running down his hands. But after Hughes had Larkins caught behind in his first over and Reid trapped Mike Atherton in front with a late in-swinger, England's top order had failed yet again. The pressure was mounting and Reid, in particular, was asking some embarrassing questions about England's batting. He was striding in more purposefully now, nerves steadied by the heat of contest.

Old hands Gower and Lamb prospered until an hour after the lunch break when Matthews was introduced. Spin on the first day at the Gabba – a welcome surprise. Matthews – cap on, shirt buttoned to the chin – was attacking, giving the ball air and staying faithful to the new techniques and philosophy he had learned in the four years since his last Test match; years in which, with the help of former Test spinners Peter Philpott and

You're out: Bruce Reid announces his return to the top with a marvellous yorker to dismiss Robin Smith.

Ashley Mallett, he had reshaped his game by becoming a genuinely attacking slow bowler.

Lamb, eager to get after Matthews's tantalising floaters, planted his feet at the crease, slashed wildly at an arm-ball that left him and was caught behind point by Hughes. Before he could regain balance, the big fast-bowler had Matthews's legs wrapped delightedly around his waist. England's in-form batsman and stand-in captain was out and Border's faith in Matthews had been repaid.

Throughout the day Gower, wafting and waving with apparent abandon, had enjoyed considerable luck. In four memorable deliveries Reid beat him outside off-stump twice, had him caught by Alderman at slip off a no-ball and beat him again. Somehow Gower was still there on 55 when Lamb went and, with the rescue-specialist Smith, had the chance to save England's innings.

In the over after Lamb's departure, Reid finally got Gower and England was 4-123. Four overs later the tall left-armer supplied the coup de grâce, bowling Smith with a stunning in-swinging yorker. That ball alone announced that Australia's bowling, so successful in England in 1989, would be even more dangerous with Reid back near his best. England was 5-134 and its destroyer of 1989, Alderman, was yet to take a wicket.

By stumps Australia was 0-16 in reply to England's 194. England cricket manager Micky Stewart stated the obvious when he said he was disappointed Gower and Lamb had not gone on from 2-117 on a wicket he thought worth at least 250. And, as if to remind England of its general misfortune, the management announced after stumps that Glamorgan opening batsman Hugh Morris had been called up on standby for Gooch.

With the wicket likely to play better in the morning, Australia held the upper hand. By stumps on the second day, there was every chance the first Test could be out of England's reach.

DAY ONE: England all out 194 (Gower 61, Lamb 32. Reid 4-53, Hughes 3-39). Australia 0-16.

IN PROFILE

Bruce Reid

Born: 14.3.63

Tests: 22. Debut v. India, Melbourne, 1985-86.

Best bowling figures: 7-51 v. England, Melbourne 1990-91.

Nickname: Chook, but I have no idea where it came from, or who thought of it. I think it might be a corruption of Bird, which I used to be called.

Favourite moment: Winning the World Cup in India in 1987.

Horror moment: When my back packed it in on the Pakistan tour of 1988.

Greatest influence: I suppose Dennis Lillee was an idol, but everyone says that. I didn't really have anyone in particular. I just picked things up along the way.

Superstitions: None at all. I'm not a superstitious cricketer.

Favourite delivery: The in-swinger to the right-hander. It creates opportunities when most of my deliveries hold their line and run across the right-hander towards the slips. The in-swinger creates uncertainty and gives you much more scope.

How do you overcome nerves? Plenty of deep breathing. As I walk back to my bowling mark I talk to myself, tell myself to relax, that it's just another game of cricket and to try to bowl like I would in a club game or a Shield game. You just have to concentrate on line and length and stay in rhythm.

Would you rather be built like Harold Larwood and a fast right-armer, or be what you are? What I am. Being a left-armer is different and that is an advantage.

Coaching tip: With bowling the thing to do is stay in rhythm and don't try to bowl like anyone else. Bowl the way that comes naturally to you.

FOR THE RECORD – DAY ONE

•This was Australia's 500th Test match.

•Wayne Larkins played his second Test on Australian soil. His first Test was at the Melbourne Cricket Ground in February 1980.

Day two

Wickets galore, scales balanced

THE ENGLISHMEN might not have batted well on day one, but on day two they showed that they could bowl and catch. In fact England did so well it earned the unexpected luxury of a 42-run first-innings lead. Unfortunately though, it left enough time in the day's play for Australia to exploit England's top-order batting weakness. At stumps, England was already 3-56 in its second innings and an extraordinary first Test was delicately poised.

During the day, 13 wickets fell for 192 runs off only 77 overs. A lamentable over rate, but an exciting day's play nonetheless.

Was the wicket that bad? Greg Chappell, an esteemed if adopted local, confirmed Waugh's earlier suspicion: 'This wicket is not the usual Test track and has always been a little uneven in pace and bounce.' The pitch had certainly seamed and the humid atmosphere had encouraged swing but, even so, on the first day the English batsmen seemed to worry themselves into a dilemma. They looked tentative, as if they were thinking about the reputation of the bowler and the vagaries of the wicket, rather than which shot to play to each delivery.

In contrast, the Australians fell while playing favourite and often productive shots, dodgy wicket or not. In 1989 those shots rarely went to hand; but this time they did. The Australian batsmen would have been telling themselves that sometimes you just have to miss out; the English bowlers that these Australians were more vulnerable than they liked to think.

Near the end, England might have been in worse trouble had Border held a straightforward catch at slip from Lamb off Hughes when the score was already 3-52. How much that dropped chance, the first by either side in two days play, would cost Australia would be known by lunch the next day. Before then, it would pay those dealing with Border to be wary. He was not a happy man.

Taylor and Marsh began Australia's innings comfortably enough but England, led by the miserly and incisive Fraser, applied pressure from the start, rarely giving away easy runs and moving the ball dangerously off the still-green wicket. So different from England's loose bowling in 1989.

Fraser trapped Marsh leg-before and then showed his cunning by going around the wicket and cramping Taylor's favourite square cut in the gully. The athletic Lewis, the best fieldsman in the England side, easily took the low catch that Taylor eventually offered. Fraser had attacked a strength but, by changing the angle, had slyly stacked the odds in his favour. In a one-on-one contest that could prove significant for the series, it was first round to the crafty Middlesex seamer.

IN PROFILE
Angus Fraser

Born: 8.8.65

Tests: 11. Debut v. Australia, Edgbaston, 1989.

Best bowling figures: 6-82 v. Australia, Melbourne, 1990-91.

Nickname: Gus, Gnats or Jacques Cousteau, after a bad round of golf once.

Favourite moment: Winning the first Test against the West Indies in Jamaica in early 1990.

Horror moment: Being hit all over the park by Salim Malik during the Nehru Cup in India in 1989.

Greatest influence: No one in particular. I've learned a lot from a lot of people. I wasn't old enough to see Lillee at his best, but I've seen quite a lot of Richard Hadlee. If I could bowl like anyone, it would be like him.

Superstitions: I like to change in the same spot at a ground where I've been successful before. Also if I've done well in a certain pair of boots I'll keep wearing them.

Favourite delivery: The ball that hits the seam and leaves the right-hander for a catch behind or in the slips. That's the most satisfying ball to bowl.

How do you overcome nerves? I'm not really a nervous sort of person as far as crowds or atmosphere go. I might get tense in certain game situations. When that happens I try to keep things simple, close irrelevant things out of my mind and concentrate on putting the ball on the spot.

Bowling philosophy: It's basically about giving them nothing, keeping the pressure on the batsmen, making them work for every run. It's a question of patience.

A tip for young pace bowlers: Bowl as much as you can and wait for the batsmen to make mistakes. Don't get bored waiting for them to get bored.

At the other end, Small took 3-6 in twelve balls. The one that got Border was a great delivery, leaving him appreciably off the wicket. Not much the batsman could do there. Boon played across the line looking to hit to leg and was out leg-before. Jones drove Lewis low to cover where Small, having a great day out, took a fine catch diving forward.

Soon after, Waugh, facing Small, cracked his favourite back-foot square drive hard but in the air to Smith at point. It was a symbolic dismissal. In 1989 on England's dry, flat batting wickets Waugh had looked invincible and that square drive was his most destructive weapon. But in the past year on Australia's bouncier, faster wickets he had struggled to control the shot. Pakistan's Wasim Akram worked him over the previous season, cramping the shot by veering in towards Waugh's rigid body. A strength was turning into a weakness and Waugh began the summer needing some big scores to secure his Test future.

In the evening session, Larkins was leg-before to Reid first ball and Atherton, looking more and more the earnest, callow youth trying to do a grown man's job, received the one all England dreads, the late outswinger from Alderman that pitches near leg and hits off. Later Alderman said he had meant to bowl exactly that delivery, adding, 'It was the same as the one that picked up Robin Smith at Lord's in 1989.' Cricketers always remember those moments when they approach perfection.

When Gower, his luck exhausted, played Hughes on, England's top three were gone. After two wonderfully see-sawing days, it was clear that the first Test wouldn't run the full distance.

What emerged on day two was the impression that England's bowlers and fieldsmen were capable of a genuine fightback. What was still unknown was whether Lamb could make Border and his team pay dearly for that dropped catch.

DAY TWO: Australia all out 152 (Matthews 35, Healy 22. Fraser 3-33, Small 3-34, Lewis 3-29). England 3-56.

IN PROFILE

Gladstone Small

Born: 18.10.61

Tests: 17. Debut v. New Zealand, Trent Bridge, 1986.

Best bowling figures: 5-48 v. Australia, Melbourne, 1986-87.

Nickname: Stony.

Favourite moment: The Melbourne Test in the 1986-87 series. I was not in the starting line-up and I was told half an hour before play that I was in the team. I took five wickets that day and later the catch (I think it was Merv Hughes in the deep off Phil Edmonds) that won the match. I won the Man of the Match award.

Horror moment: Bowling an eighteen-ball over at Coventry in a county championship match against Middlesex, in 1982 I think. The funniest moment was when I ran off two paces to bowl the seventeenth and what should have been the last ball and bowled a wide. That was very funny. The record is twenty balls in an over. If I'd known that I would have done it. At that stage two more wouldn't have mattered.

Greatest influence: From a bowling point of view, the two guys who helped me when I started at Warwickshire, David Brown and Bob Willis. They helped me on the mental side of things and how to work batsmen out.

Superstitions: None whatsoever. I don't understand how people can have them. Batsmen tend to have them more than bowlers.

Favourite delivery: The dream ball. The one that pitches around leg stump, moves late and hits the top of off-stump.

How do you overcome nerves? They go as soon as I get on the field and get the ball in my hand. You always feel some apprehension beforehand; I'd call anyone a liar who says they don't get nervous before playing. People handle them differently. Some people sweat a lot or whatever. I go to sleep.

Coaching tip: Be yourself and be relaxed. That's basically it.

Comeback: David Gower where he likes it – as an integral part of the England team. A timely 150 in the last Test of the winter ensured selection for his fourth Ashes tour, after a year which had seen him dumped as England captain and missing selection for the West Indies tour.

Gower's poser: Where's the enemy?

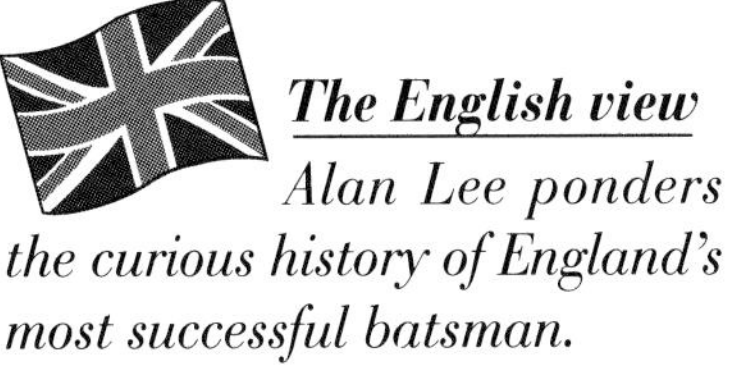

The English view

Alan Lee ponders the curious history of England's most successful batsman.

IN THE PAST two cricketing decades, only two English players have polarised the public. Geoffrey Boycott and Ian Botham provoked extremes of abuse and adulation, not so much because they were great cricketers (which, unanimously, they were) but because they were somehow larger than life. In their behaviour, both on and off the field, they were perceived either as hugely appealing or utterly appalling. Now there is a third Englishman who fits the bill in David Gower, and early in the day it became evident that his character and his contributions would be recurring themes of this tour.

Gower has grown accustomed to the perverse way in which we treat our major sporting stars. It no longer surprises him to be portrayed as a Goliath one day and a goon the next. Such fickleness would have been more irksome on this tour, however, for he carried the burden of many vocal opinions that he was not entitled to be there. After the first Test, those detractors were temporarily silenced. Included at number three in England's side despite his traditionally sketchy start to a tour, he top-scored in each innings. England lost, and ultimately lost badly, but the most convenient scapegoat was unavailable.

Gower is often misunderstood – just like Graham Gooch, but for the very opposite reason. Gooch is forever being accused of looking miserable; Gower's sunny demeanour has invited many a charge of carelessness. There is, of course, middle ground in both cases and if some feel Gooch would improve for smiling a shade more, and others think Gower would do better not to smile quite so often, they both care deeply about their cricket but have their own, singular ways of showing it.

To some extent, Gower still bears the scars of the 1989 English summer, when he was recalled as captain by the new chairman of England's cricket committee, Ted Dexter, and plunged from a widely shared air of a new dawn to the dark depression that accompanied a 4-0 defeat by Australia. It was a summer in which many things were botched, not least the way in which Gower left the job. He meant to resign, changed his mind for reasons he now finds hard to quantify, and so was inevitably sacked. Then, as if one public humiliation was not sufficient for him, Gower was dropped from the team to tour the Caribbean.

Briefly, it shattered him. With acceptance of his lot came the motivation for change. And how he changed his life. He called it his 'everything must go' period, and everything went – the only county club he had ever played for, the woman with whom he had lived for years, his home and

GOWER'S GOONS

Pathetic England are slaughtered on dream track

ASHES '89

HEADINGLEY: TRIUMPH IN '81 . . . AND HORROR IN '89

HOW I EIGHT THEM!

DEXTER WASN'T THERE

Over the top: A London tabloid attack on David Gower and his team during Australia's successful 1989 tour of England. Gower's critics were quieter during the 1990-91 series.

roots. He joined Hampshire and, rather sooner than expected, won back his England place. It was not, at once, a rich reunion and the knives were being sharpened for him again ... when his sense of self-preservation produced a century in his final Test innings of the summer.

Not only was this enough to secure his place on the tour he has always enjoyed most, it was also enough to demonstrate the massive public support that Gower commands. With the demise of Ian Botham he is beyond doubt the most popular cricketer in England: charmingly urbane at almost all times and a peerless strokeplayer to watch. Most of the nation celebrated for him, but reservations remained elsewhere. Was he still good enough? Would he be properly motivated? And what would be the influence of his habitually languid ways on players educated with the all-action regime of Gooch and Stewart?

Making 61 and 27 at the Gabba partly answered questions one and two. Although he might have been out to almost any ball in his first half-hour's batting, in the second innings he rose to a plane above most of his team-mates. He was motivated, because this was a Test match, and Test cricket always brings out the best in Gower. But having risen to that occasion, the sensitive third question remained unanswered. How would he react in the aftermath of defeat?

Gower has found it increasingly difficult to mask his contempt for one-day cricket and, as England attempted to regroup after a Test which started poorly, improved dramatically and ended shambolically, one-day cricket was all they had to sustain them. Ten limited-overs games in the next three weeks was not at all what they needed, and yet it would be a critical period of the tour for confidence and morale.

Gower, the senior professional and the most closely scrutinised member of the party, had a major role to play, like it or not. For after their collapse in Brisbane the options were to rally impressively or come apart at the seams.

Day three

Suddenly, it's all over

ON THE THIRD day batsmen finally got their turn to excel on Brisbane's challenging wicket, but only two managed to master it and both, unexpectedly, were Australians.

Poor old England lasted a mere 33.1 overs, losing its last seven wickets for a paltry 58. It was a collapse that rivalled any of the horrors of 1989. And to make matters worse, Alderman did the damage, finishing with a career-best 6-47 and deepening even further the fear he instils in English hearts every time he saunters in off that harmless-looking run.

The Englishmen's reluctance to counter-attack Alderman again cost them dearly. Lamb started positively, pulling a not-so-short one for four in the first over of the day. That was the stuff England needed, someone to show that if you attacked Alderman he would not be as great a danger. The theory is that it is better to leave the crease to a swing bowler like Alderman, to hit him down the ground rather than defend from the crease and so allow the ball the maximum time to deviate.

Alderman is a deceptive bowler. In person he is taller and broader than expected and from twenty yards away in a Test match he is quicker than he looks from the fence, quick enough to force batsmen to make instant decisions. Before his shoulder injury in 1982-83 he was quite sharp and had a good bouncer. Now, like an ageing artist, he has simplified his work, honed his bowling down to the basics.

Alderman nags away at the stumps, moving the ball just enough each time. That grimace that passes for a smile, which he wears as he runs in, suggests to batsmen that he knows all their fears and weaknesses. Alderman asks questions about the batsman's temperament and skill every time he bowls; in contrast, when Devon Malcolm charges in, the questions turn back on the bowler. Alderman wears away at batsmen's nerves, forcing them to make critical decisions every ball. When a batsman knows a fatal misjudgement can come off any delivery, he is under extreme pressure. Alderman knows that and thrives on it, like a polite but determined interrogator.

Hence the theory of getting to Alderman before he gets to you. But a batsman needs footwork and shots to do this and Lamb, this time, was simply not good enough. In his third over of the day, Alderman trapped him in front with that sliding ball that spears in from off to hit the pads with unerring accuracy. This on top of the one that bowled Atherton the evening before must have caused apoplexy in the England camp. 'Here we go again ...'

Surprisingly Smith failed for the second time in the game, driving too early at Alderman to be caught at mid-on. It was not an unplayable ball like the one from Reid in the first innings. This dismissal was the result of half an hour of sustained Test match pressure.

Despite the redoubtable Russell and some supporting resistance from Lewis and Small, England was all out for 114, leaving Australia 157 to win in 50 overs on the third afternoon, with two more days available if needed.

Ominously, England's bowlers looked a far less dangerous lot in the second innings. With the buzz of imminent victory wafting across from an increasingly expectant crowd, Marsh and Taylor played comfortably. In the end they reached the target at a canter, with four overs (and two days) to spare.

The Australian openers finally brought some sanity to this extraordinary match. After thirty wickets had fallen for a mere 460 runs, they looked like they had settled in to bat for another two days. Taylor failed in the first innings yet still came out of the game with his Test average

IN PROFILE

Geoff Marsh

Born: 31.12.58

Tests: 41. Debut v. India, Adelaide, 1985-86.

Highest Score: 138 v. England, Trent Bridge, 1989.

Nickname: Swampy.

Favourite moment: I'd have to say winning the Ashes at Old Trafford in 1989. After that, the parade in Sydney and the overall reception when we got home were a great surprise, as we didn't realise the interest there had been.

Horror moment: After such a great year, losing the Test against New Zealand in Wellington in 1990.

Greatest influence: There have been quite a few people along the way. Jim Watkins coached me from my school days, and Darryl Foster and Bob Simpson have also helped a lot.

Superstitions: The only one I have is that I always put my right pad on first. I don't know why.

Favourite shot: I suppose the cover drive and the square cut. But what I enjoy most is when I get one away with a shot I don't normally play as well as those two.

How do you overcome nerves? I'm still trying to find out. I enjoy getting nervous because nerves mean I'm right mentally. If I wasn't nervous I'd be worried. Every sportsman, even Allan Border, gets nervous. It's just something you learn to cope with as you gain more experience.

Coaching tip: As a youngster I think you should learn all the shots and just enjoy the game. Don't worry too much about technique, just enjoy playing the game.

Nice view: Greg Matthews watches the concluding stages of the Test. It was his first Test for Australia since 1986.

improved. His second innings 67 not out left him with an average of 65.19 from 29 innings. In Wisden's all-time list you need a minimum of twenty innings to qualify. Taylor now lay a clear second to Bradman, and nearly five runs ahead of his nearest rival, the South African genius, Graeme Pollock. The others on that list of Test averages are all accepted as greats. So, how great is Mark Taylor?

The Man of the Match was Alderman. At the press conference he said he had been motivated by two factors. One was his annoyance with criticism that is sometimes levelled at him. 'Everyone says I am a WACA bowler or an England bowler who can't bowl a hoop down George St (Sydney) or Stanley St (Brisbane),' he said. 'It has always been a big thing in the back of my mind. It is very annoying, but I think I'm slowly getting rid of the reputation now.'

Alderman's other motivation was the threat that his captain was about to revert to his infamous 'Captain Grumpy' days. Only Border's teammates know what that can mean. Border had been very annoyed about dropping Lamb the previous evening and in Alderman's view that was enough to lift all the bowlers to an extra special effort.

Border confirmed that he hadn't slept much the night before. 'I dropped the ball another two hundred times. You always think of the worst possible scenario at moments like that and I had visions of standing out there at five o'clock with Lamb 180 not out. Coming to the match this morning I was really on edge.'

Border need not have worried. England's batting was not good enough to take that advantage and Australia had beaten England by an innings in three days for the first time since 1938.

For England, it was the worst possible start.

DAY THREE: England all out 114 (Gower 27). Australia 0-157 (Marsh 72 not out, Taylor 67 not out).
RESULT: Australia won by 10 wickets
MAN OF THE MATCH: Terry Alderman (Australia)

FOR THE RECORD – DAY THREE

•Allan Lamb passed 4000 Test runs, the seventeenth Englishman to achieve this milestone.

•Allan Border went to the batting crease for the 200th time. Only Sunil Gavaskar (India) had played more Test innings (214 innings in 125 Tests).

•England totalled 114, its lowest Test score ever in Brisbane. Its previous lowest was 122, in 1950-51.

•Terry Alderman returned his best Test bowling figures (6/47), his previous best being 6/128 against England at Lord's in 1989. Alderman's 6/47 was the fourteenth time that he had taken five wickets or more in a Test innings. This was only the fourth time he had done so in Australia.

More of the same: Another Test against England, another Australian victory. Merv Hughes gets close to his captain Allan Border. Jones, Boon, Waugh, Reid and Matthews enjoy it their way.

Man of the Match: Terry Alderman wiped out England, and knocked over a few critics on the way.

FOR THE RECORD – FIRST TEST

•Peter Cantrell took two catches while acting as 'substitute' in England's second innings. Of the six occasions when an Australian substitute fieldsman has taken two catches in an innings, three of those have been at the Woolloongabba ground in Brisbane.

•Terry Alderman moved into tenth position on the list of wicket-takers for Australia in Test cricket with 161 wickets.

•Australia recorded its third Test victory by ten wickets after trailing on the first innings. The other occasions were at Birmingham, 1909 and Georgetown, 1972-73.

•Australia won the Test inside three days. It was the first time they had defeated England inside three days since the third Test of 1938 at Headingley. (In 1950-51 Australia won a Test in three days, however there was a day washed out due to rain.)

A débâcle for England

'The fact is that we didn't play well enough and our batting let us down,' said a subdued Lamb.

IN BRISBANE, England threw away what might have been its best chance the whole summer to overcome the confident locals.

When England's bowlers managed to give their undeserving and ultimately ungrateful batsmen a 42-run first-innings lead, even a reasonable second-innings total would have given them something to bowl to in the fourth innings, and some chance of a win. That England was beaten by an innings after leading on the first was a crushing blow. It was unlikely its bowlers would find a wicket as helpful as the one at the Gabba until they got to Perth for the fifth Test in February. And by then it would possibly be too late.

In 1989, England did not have one day when it clearly outplayed Australia. That was in six Tests. In Brisbane it was one-all after two days, and yet England failed to take the chance for a win that its bowlers provided and Australia steamrolled to a devastating innings win.

Good teams need only one sniff of victory. Australia, let off the hook, went on to win well. England, on this evidence, did not look good enough.

For Australia, the momentum gathered on the England tour in 1989 had been maintained and the opposition immediately reminded of its weaknesses. The game ended with a disheartening dose of déjà vu for England – Alderman taking wickets and Taylor making runs. Ashes 1989 all over again?

At the end of the first Test the question was whether England could recover. The most common reply was that unless the batsmen began to bat correctly, it was doubtful. The conditions were not like those they had experienced in their recent summer. They were not facing pop-gun medium-pacers on the flattest of flat batting strips where they could plant the front foot in the same spot to every ball, whatever its line, and hit more in expectation than hope. In Australia they were facing a better pace attack than the one that had destroyed them in 1989 and on wickets that were less forgiving of technical flaws.

Reid added enormous penetration and variety to Border's attack. He is world class. Contrary to the popular image, Hughes was using brain as well as brawn and, by lunch on the third day, Alderman had destroyed England once already in the series. The Australians' pace bowling reserves were strong. If the England openers could not dig in soon, it would be too late.

As a subdued Lamb noted after the game: 'Getting bowled out for 114 just wasn't on. The pitch played well and we didn't bat well. There's nothing more to it than that. We didn't look like taking a wicket when Australia batted this afternoon and that rubs salt into the wound... It was a good toss to win but that's not the point. The fact is that we didn't play well enough and our batting let us down.'

England's bowling, although successful in the first-innings rout, had its problems too. Devon Malcolm took one wicket and rarely caused trouble. Bowling fast is handy, but Malcolm was bowling to batsmen not unused to pace. They wouldn't be bluffed by any hype surrounding England's supposed new spearhead.

Border agreed it had been a strange match. 'I can't recall a Test quite like it. Normally if you win in three days you have blitzed them from the word go. I don't know where the smart money was going last night but I thought it was pretty evenly poised.' As for the wicket, Border noted: 'A three-day Test usually means a nightmare track but the quality wasn't that bad.'

England's batting was though, and that was the game.

Happy Jack: The Gabba's most famous character salutes the Australian dressing-rooms as victory nears.

FOR THE RECORD – BATTING

•Mark Taylor's average increased to 65.19.

Highest batting averages

(Minimum 20 innings)

Batsman	Country	M	Inns	Runs	Avrge
DG Bradman	Australia	52	80	6996	99.94
MA Taylor	Australia	16	29	1695	65.19
RG Pollock	South Africa	23	41	2256	60.97
GA Headley	West Indies	22	40	2190	60.83
H Sutcliffe	England	54	84	4555	60.73

•Mark Taylor and Geoff Marsh's opening partnership of 157 was a record against England in Brisbane. The previous record was 136, made by Bill Lawry and Bob Simpson in 1962-63.

•Unfinished opening partnerships by Australians:

WH Ponsford & A Jackson	172	against West Indies,	Adelaide,	1930-31
MA Taylor & GR Marsh	157	against England,	Brisbane,	1990-91
KR Stackpole & IR Redpath	135	against West Indies,	Georgetown,	1972-73

The First Test
(Test no. 1156)

Australia v. England
Woolloongabba, Brisbane
23, 24, 25 November 1990

Toss:
Australia

Twelfth men:
CG Rackemann (Australia);
EE Hemmings (England)

Umpires:
AR Crafter;
PJ McConnell

Result:
Australia won by 10 wickets

Man of the Match:
TM Alderman (Australia)

Attendance:
32,321

ENGLAND

FIRST INNINGS

Batsman	How Out	Ttl	Balls	Mins	4s	6s
MA Atherton	lbw Reid	13	54	91	–	–
W Larkins	c Healy b Hughes	12	37	42	1	–
DI Gower	c Healy b Reid	61	121	162	8	–
AJ Lamb (C)	c Hughes b Matthews	32	78	106	5	–
RA Smith	b Reid	7	13	20	–	–
AJ Stewart	lbw Reid	4	17	22	1	–
RC Russell (+)	c & b Alderman	16	74	93	2	–
CC Lewis	c Border b Hughes	20	31	44	3	1
GC Small	not out	12	35	57	1	–
ARC Fraser	c Healy b Alderman	1	5	8	–	–
DE Malcolm	c Waugh b Hughes	5	7	8	1	–
SUNDRIES	1b, 7lb, 0w, 3nb	11	472	331	22	1
TOTAL		**194**				
FALL	**23 43 117 123 134 135 167 181 187 194**					

BOWLING

Bowler	Overs	Mdn	Runs	Wkts	NB	W
Alderman	18	5	44	2	–	–
Reid	18	3	53	4	2	–
Hughes	19	5	39	3	1	–
Waugh	7	2	20	–	–	–
Matthews	16	8	30	1	–	–
OVERS	**78**					

SECOND INNINGS

Batsman	How Out	Ttl	Balls	Mins	4s	6s
MA Atherton	b Alderman	15	44	64	1	–
W Larkins	lbw Reid	0	1	6	–	–
DI Gower	b Hughes	27	44	63	2	–
AJ Lamb (C)	lbw Alderman	14	24	32	2	–
RC Russell (+)	lbw Waugh	15	84	116	1	–
RA Smith	c Taylor b Alderman	1	14	34	–	–
AJ Stewart	c sub (PE Cantrell) b Alderman	6	10	16	–	–
CC Lewis	lbw Alderman	14	47	71	–	–
GC Small	c Alderman b Hughes	15	42	54	1	–
ARC Fraser	c sub (PE Cantrell) b Alderman	0	8	14	–	–
DE Malcolm	not out	0	5	5	–	–
SUNDRIES	0b, 3lb, 0w, 4nb	7	323	242	7	–
TOTAL		**114**				
FALL	**0 42 46 60 78 84 93 112 114 114**					

BOWLING

Bowler	Overs	Mdn	Runs	Wkts	NB	W
Alderman	22	7	47	6	1	–
Reid	14	3	40	1	1	–
Hughes	12.1	5	17	2	2	–
Matthews	1	1	0	–	–	–
Waugh	4	2	7	1	–	–
OVERS	**53.1**					

AUSTRALIA

FIRST INNINGS

Batsman	How Out	Ttl	Balls	Mins	4s	6s
GR Marsh	lbw Fraser	9	31	29	1	–
MA Taylor	c Lewis b Fraser	10	44	69	1	–
DC Boon	lbw Small	18	42	85	–	–
AR Border (C)	c Atherton b Small	9	30	33	1	–
DM Jones	c Small b Lewis	17	42	65	2	–
SR Waugh	c Smith b Small	1	4	7	–	–
GRJ Matthews	c Small b Malcolm	35	93	127	2	–
IA Healy (+)	c Atherton b Lewis	22	71	110	2	–
MG Hughes	c Russell b Fraser	9	23	23	1	–
BA Reid	b Lewis	0	8	9	–	–
TM Alderman	not out	0	3	4	–	–
SUNDRIES	lb, 10lb, 0w, 11nb	22	391	285	10	–
TOTAL		**152**				
FALL	**22 35 49 60 64 89 135 150 150 152**					

BOWLING

Bowler	Overs	Mdn	Runs	Wkts	NB	W
Malcolm	17	2	45	1	3	–
Fraser	21	6	33	3	5	–
Small	16	4	34	3	–	–
Lewis	9	–	29	3	3	–
OVERS	**63**					

SECOND INNINGS

Batsman	How Out	Ttl	Balls	Mins	4s	6s
MA Taylor	not out	67	139	197	7	–
GR Marsh	not out	72	154	197	9	–
SUNDRIES	3b, 2lb, 3w, 10nb	18	293	197	16	–
TOTAL	**0 wkts for**	**157**				

BOWLING

Bowler	Overs	Mdn	Runs	Wkts	NB	W
Fraser	14	2	49	–	1	–
Small	15	2	36	–	1	3
Malcolm	9	5	22	–	1	–
Lewis	6	–	29	–	7	–
Atherton	2	–	16	–	–	–
OVERS	**46**					

The theory of positivity

From the square
David Gower peers through the gloom and sees a positive future.

"IN THE RUN-UP to the first Test England appeared to be on much the same course as on its last tour of Australia in 1986-87. Neither time did it show much corrective form, but at least in 1986 all that changed from the first day of the series, and the tour went on to be one of England's most successful ever.

The bad news in 1990 was that it was Australia's turn to win the first Test and England's woes did not miraculously disappear at the sight of a proper game of cricket, even though there had been cause for some optimism when it earned a first-innings lead through an apparently brilliant bowling and fielding display.

When, a day later, the Test was comprehensively lost, the problem for the captain and management was what to do next, and, quite rightly, they opted first for a day off to reflect on what had happened and to allow bodies to relax and recover as well. Cynics may say that a side cannot be tired after a quick three-day Test, but there had been precious little genuinely free time in the previous month.

At a time like this many of the problems are mental. It has been said a million times, but I am a firm believer that confidence is as big an asset to a player and a team as pure ability and talent. In the aftermath of a decisive Test defeat work has to be done on the skills of the players in a way that confirms both their belief in themselves and the confidence of others in their ability. Part of the answer is to try to concentrate on the positive aspects of what has just happened – some times more easily done than at others! As such, the way the bowlers performed and the fielders supported them on the second day made England look like a side that had been unbeaten for two years! The hard part then was to explain how exactly the same personnel allowed the Australians to cruise to a ten-wicket win, even allowing for the fact that the wicket was playing at its best and that the run of the ball had deserted the touring side and changed allegiance to the hosts – without ignoring the fact that Marsh and Taylor also played well.

So it was back to the nets forty-eight hours after, with the plan being to work on specific vital areas. However, whatever efforts were to be made outside the matches, what England needed most was a line of confident top-order batsmen to post proper totals. Runs on the board always give a side confidence and allow bowlers to operate without the feeling that every single run is absolutely crucial and that they are solely responsible for drawing the side back into a game.

Batting in Australia is sometimes a problem for English batsmen; traditionally it is a question of adapting to bouncier wickets. But the Brisbane pitch was neither pacey nor bouncy and the England batsmen had more to think about the various styles of Reid and Alderman when analysing their mistakes and preparing for the next contest.

Unfortunately the schedule meant a month of one-day matches and one four-day match before the second Test. The idea would be win a few of those to regain some confidence all round and perhaps for a few batsmen to get some runs on the board with the fielders spread further afield.

The one thing not to do was to believe all the gloom, doom and despair being printed in Fleet Street, but to remember the positive form that had earned each player his right to be in Australia. ”

Back in charge: Graham Gooch, injured hand heavily bandaged, returned to the fray in the match against the Bradman XI in Bowral.

INTERLUDE

29 NOVEMBER – 25 DECEMBER 1990

The one-day games

Some interlude! England's form went from bad to worse and the injury list grew and grew.

AFTER ITS three-day thrashing in the first Test, England had a chance to pull together over the next three weeks with the first series of one-day internationals. And with any luck its captain, Graham Gooch, would be back in play some time during that period before the second Test started in Melbourne on Boxing Day.

Two years earlier against the West Indies Australia had lost the first three Tests but was able to use a similar programme of one-dayers to regain confidence and go on to win the fourth Test in Sydney and draw the fifth in Adelaide. Soon after, the Australians had left for their supremely successful 1989 Ashes tour of England.

However, a similar opportunity was just wasted by Gooch's men. England lost matches, players lost form, and the injury list kept growing.

After the Brisbane Test, allegations surfaced that England's acting captain, Allan Lamb, had been at a Gold Coast casino, some distance from Brisbane, late on the night before he was due to resume his second-innings rescue operation on the third day of the Test. Lamb had gone to the casino with the rather noticeable trio of the very rich media magnate Kerry Packer, the very tall television commentator Tony Greig and the very popular team-mate David Gower. The next day Lamb was out in the first over of play and England duly collapsed with familar aplomb.

For a few days admissions and explanations followed early denials by the England camp. It was another unnecessary bit of bother on a disaster-prone tour.

After badly losing its first one-day match, against New Zealand, England travelled to the national capital, Canberra, for the now traditional game against the Prime Minister's XI. At the official reception the evening before the match, a smiling Gower was photographed with the PM, Bob Hawke. The next morning in a major newspaper, above the picture, was a typically light-hearted quote from Gower. 'In the Kiwi game I felt super, in magic form ... for all four balls.' Gower, as usual, was still finding life amusing, but the rest of the touring party must have been sinking deeper into depression.

England lost the PM's game by 31 runs against a team of young hopefuls bolstered by three Test players: Border, McDermott and Veletta. The British press was suitably scathing in its response. The London *Sun's* Ian Todd wrote: 'The Aussie crowd just could not believe the imcompetence of England's ramshackle bunch of no-hopers as their Ashes tour turned to disaster.' The headline in the *Daily Express* was: 'Shabby Poms fit only for sack race'.

The tourists rallied briefly to beat New Zealand in a one-day game before losing comprehensively to Australia and then going to Bowral, the country town in southern New South Wales where Sir Donald Bradman spent his boyhood.

Despite the long-awaited return of skipper Gooch, Old Blighty's finest reached a new level of incompetence. England lost by seven wickets with forty-seven balls to spare to a bowling and fielding side that was every bit as ragged as England but, unlike England, did have only five first-class players in it.

Innocent onlooker: Allan Lamb rests his torn calf muscle as his team-mates take the field in Ballarat without him.

The home team's captain, former great Australian batsman Doug Walters, summoned all his country-bred powers of understatement to opine that: 'I don't think Graham Gooch would be very impressed with the boys.' He wasn't. Gooch gave his team a real blast after the match.

And while the London *Sun's* headline this time screamed: 'The shame old story', England cricket supremo Ted Dexter assured Britain that there was no need for panic. 'They are all trying like hell and I am satisfied they are doing their best,' he said.

In all England won two of its six one-day international games in this period, both wins against the Kiwis. Its embarrassment against the Australians reached a high in Brisbane on 16 December when the master of the one-day game, Dean Jones, thrashed a stunning 145 during which he treated Gooch's attack with brutal disdain.

By the time England reached colonial Ballarat in rural Victoria for its only four-day match between the first and second Tests, things were ready to fall into complete disarray. And they did.

At one stage on the first day, Victoria was 1-300, with opener Warren Ayres and Dean Jones both making hundreds. Jones continued his demolition of England's bowlers and said later: 'I always knew I was going to get a hundred. I wanted to keep the pressure on their bowlers.'

England scrambled a draw from the Ballarat game but Lamb, Morris, Gooch, Gower and Small all suffered injuries. Gooch and Gower were expected to be fit for the Test; Lamb and Small were almost certain to miss out.

There had been no turn-around for England during the interlude.

Dean Jones: one-day superstar

The world's best: Dean Jones salutes the crowd during another of his brilliant one-day innings.

ASK ANY BOY or girl at a one-day international these days what they have come to see and he or she will say the same thing: Dean Jones smashing the ball out of the ground. Jones is not only the best one-day batsman in the world but, in Australia, has now come to epitomise the best of the one-day game. Showmanship, brilliant athleticism and daring strokeplay.

Jones is a player more prone to highs and lows than most. He thrives on adrenalin and confidence. When he is on a high, he soars way above others. When he is struggling he can sink lower than anyone of comparable ability. In his early career he batted on pure instinct and, inclined to live life on the edge, often tried too hard to attack. Now in his mature years, Jones has found a better balance between natural exuberance and the more calculated approach required by such a demanding and variable game as Test cricket.

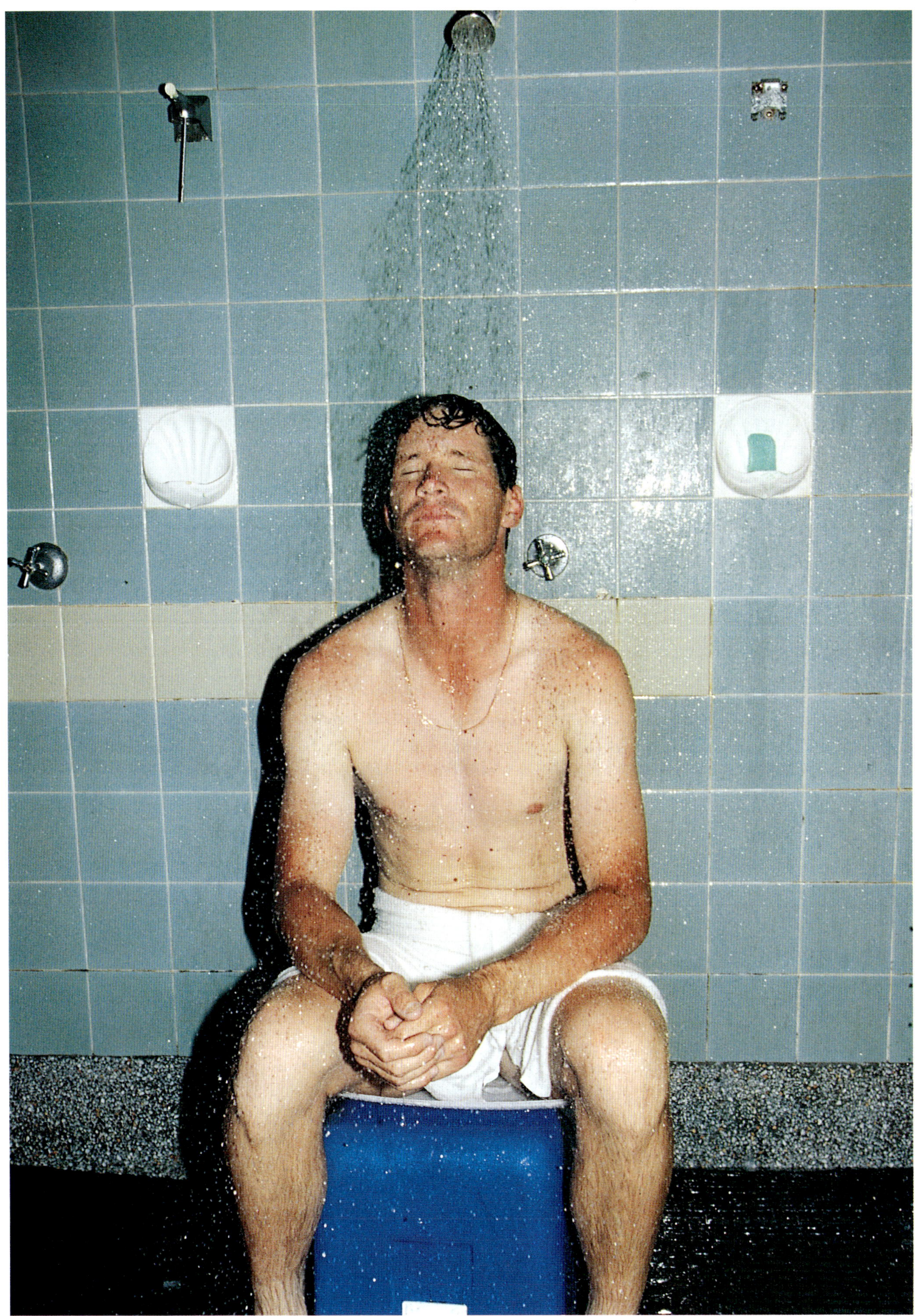

Hot stuff: Dean Jones reflects on the the hustle and bustle of the limited overs game.

IN PROFILE
Dean Jones

Born: 24.3.61

Tests: 39. Debut v. West Indies, Trinidad, 1983-84.

Highest score: 216 v. West Indies, Adelaide, 1988-89.

Nickname: Deano.

Favourite moment: There have to be two. Winning the Ashes series in England in 1989 and winning the World Cup final in Calcutta in 1987.

Horror moment: Making a pair at Lahore in 1988 in the third Test against Pakistan. Also any loss.

Greatest influence: Keith Stackpole and John Scholes when I was young and, for the past five years, Bob Simpson.

Superstitions: I always put my left pad on first and I always wear something new.

Favourite shot: Anything that scores runs. I suppose my favourite shots are the ones through the on-side.

How do you overcome nerves? By doing a lot of exercises, especially deep breathing, and by talking to myself.

Coaching tip: Use a light bat, play straight, and watch and learn from the best in the world.

But in the hyped-up atmosphere of the one-day game, Jones is freed from most of these demands and has all the scope he needs to invent shots, entertain crowds and infuriate bowlers and fieldsmen. Jones's presence creates much of that intense atmosphere and he is in turn carried along by it, the one feeding off the other.

During a bad slump in 1988-89 which cost him his Test place, it was the one-day games sandwiched between Tests that helped him regain form. Since then, he has been on a permanent high. In both Test cricket and one-day games he averages just below 50 – quite a remarkable achievement, particularly in the latter, given the limited time allowed for one-day innings.

As well as producing brilliant strokeplay, Jones must now be the best runner-between-wickets in the world. Perhaps ever. His aggressive running this summer was one of the highlights of the series, electrifying for spectators and destructive for his opponents. Jones also uses his sprinting speed in the field where, during the past few years, he has perfected a method of diving towards the fence to save boundaries – a thrill for the crowds – which rarely results in even a minor injury. Jones also has a powerful arm and delights in showing it. A favourite is throwing from the deep over the bowler's head to the keeper at the far end.

Many of the Australians have adopted Jones's fielding methods if not all his exuberant mannerisms. He has developed techniques that have taken one-day cricket further along the road to perfection. In years to come Dean Jones will be looked on as something of a pioneer.

An early Jones mentor, Keith Stackpole, has said of Jones that he approaches batting with a fast bowler's aggressive temperament. Jones destroyed England in that breath-taking 145 in Brisbane and less than a week later did the same on the first day of the four-day Victoria v. England match at Ballarat. In both innings he was particularly severe on swing-bowler Martin Bicknell. When he came off after his hundred at Ballarat, he is said to have remarked to team-mates: 'I've got Bicknell stuffed now. He doesn't know where to bowl to me.'

A formidable opponent, Dean Jones ... and a wonderfully exciting cricketer.

The boy from Bowral

From the square

David Gower imagines how the Don would have fared in modern-day cricket.

"FEW TOWNS have the same sense of history as Bowral, in New South Wales, where we stopped between one-day internationals in December. Bowral is the town where Sir Donald Bradman grew up and began learning the game that made him a genuine sporting legend. The word 'legend' is often tagged to people who barely deserve the title; but in the case of the Don, it is not overstating his cricketing feats. After all, a batsman who manages to average 99.94 in a Test career is more than just a fairly good player. The simple fact that his statistics outstripped any of his contemporaries shows the measure of the man in comparison with his peers.

Inevitably the question is posed, 'How would the Don have fared in modern cricket?' There can be little doubt that his talents would have flourished in any era, whatever changes there might have been in attitudes, fielding standards, bowling attacks or even over rates. However, this much is certain: that with the lesser number of balls delivered daily in the modern game, he would have struggled to accumulate his totals at the same rapid pace.

Compare the bowling attacks of different eras and we run into the impossible task of judging, for instance, the pace and hostility of Larwood and his cohorts during the Bodyline furore against the not dissimilar tactics of the West Indian sides in recent years. Again it would be churlish to suggest anything but that Bradman would have succeeded. Even one-day cricket should not have been a problem for him, whatever his thoughts might be on the proliferation of that aspect of our game.

The ground and museum at Bowral are a wonderful compliment to Bradman. Sadly, on our day there he was unable to be present. Sadly, also, England failed to win the game we had gone to Bowral to play, that honour being accorded to the next generation of aspiring Australian country-born cricketers, who displayed no little talent.

The home of the legend: The plaque outside the house in Bowral where the young Don Bradman spent his boyhood.

It will be interesting in, say, fifty years time to see how the comparisons will be made between Bradman, the legend, Gavaskar, the world's leading Test run scorer, and Border, Australia's current hero and a man whom I have at least been able to watch from close quarters and admire over the last decade or so. Given all the discrepancies I have touched on, it is still significant to compare the basic figures, with Border's average in the mid-fifties, extraordinary by modern standards and over the best part of a hundred and twenty Test matches, still a long way short of the Don's.

As to character, I have met the Don a handful of times at the Adelaide Oval and exchanged polite greetings. It is hard to imagine the deeds performed by this small and apparently mild man with none of the bluster of many modern cricketers, but I have no doubt about his inner steel. Anyone who can go out and make the runs he did and with such frequency has my bemused admiration."

Toiler: Angus Fraser bowled his heart (and his body) out from the southern end. His reward? A career-best 6-82, and a standing ovation from the crowd.

THE SECOND TEST

26 – 30 DECEMBER 1990

The festive season meant nothing to Border. 'If we get our chance we are going to nail them.'

ENGLAND'S frustration at its long list of injuries boiled over on the evening before the second Test when the usually mild-mannered David Gower walked out of the Melbourne Cricket Ground nets after prying television cameras interfered with a fitness test he was trying to conduct.

Gower's bruised wrist was the last of a series of injuries that had affected England's squad significantly in the fortnight before the Melbourne Test match. Allan Lamb and Gladstone Small had already been ruled out for the Test with serious muscle strains when, on the last day of the match against Victoria at Ballarat, both Graham Gooch and Gower suffered bruising to their hands during a fast and hostile spell of bowling from Merv Hughes. When England left Ballarat, only two days before the Test, both Gooch and Gower were also in doubt.

Surely England's luck had not deserted it to such an extent that it would be without its three most senior batsmen and its most experienced bowler for the crucial match in Melbourne. Given Gooch's reputation for faithfulness to the cause, it was still likely he would be tossing the coin with Allan Border at 10.30am on Boxing Day. If not, England had little hope.

Gower, top-scorer for England in both innings in the first Test, would have been encouraged by the thought that the match in Melbourne would probably be his last Test appearance at the MCG. He is a player with a sense of the theatrics of the game and would have been keen to bat out in that distant, lonely middle one more time.

Gower may appear the most relaxed, laid-back cricketer of them all, but that is a cliché that has attached itself to him because of his easy, smiling manner. The truth is very different. Friends say he is anything but a romantic. Just as Test cricket is a much more physically dangerous and demanding game than it appears from the boundary, so Gower is a tougher, more calculated character than his appearance suggests. No one scores seven thousand Test runs by being casual. It is too hard a game for that.

Gower explains: 'For ten years people have been using that tag: casual and laid-back. Every now and then I take the time to rebuff it slightly. I'm sure a lot of people think it's true. After a certain run in Test cricket there's got to be a lot more to it than that. No one just walks out there and coolly turns it on. Everyone has to build himself up in some way.'

Odd view: The gaping hole in the MCG left by workers rebuilding the huge Southern Stand.

Appearances are rarely accurate reflections of reality. Gower admits that the celebrated smiling, sunny disposition is often a convenient defence mechanism, a cover for the deeper, more disturbed moods that afflict all cricketers. 'Sometimes you have to make a more conscious use of it than at other times,' he says.

While England and the famous Melbourne sporting public waited to see whether Gower would play the second Test, the Australian camp had its own injury scare when Terry Alderman pulled up sore after the Sheffield Shield match against New South Wales in Perth. Although he was not able to stretch out fully in the nets prior to the match, something the wily old pro never does anyway, Alderman was nevertheless expected to play. Craig McDermott was flown to Melbourne just in case.

Border, despite the festive season, promised England no mercy. 'I've played enough cricket to know that when you are given an opportunity like this, you have to make the most of it,' he said after the Christmas Day practice session. 'If we get our chance we are going to nail them.'

Resting up: Terry Alderman receives ice treatment for a strained groin muscle.

England's best hope seemed to be for Gooch to win the toss and send Australia in on one of those green and moist first-day wickets the MCG had served up in recent series. But a glance at the pale, flat wicket on Christmas Day revealed that the bowlers from both sides would be in for some hard, slogging work.

All Australia needed to do was continue its good form. England, without Gladstone Small and Chris Lewis, the latter already packing his bags for home after stress fractures in his back had been confirmed, had to bowl as well or better than it did in the first innings in Brisbane when it took an unexpected first-innings lead.

The England batting was always going to be the major problem. Gooch, despite a lack of match practice, would help. Whether or not he could inspire more resolution from his batting colleagues would determine the result of the match.

FOR THE RECORD – DAY ONE

- Allan Border led Australia for the twentieth consecutive time against England, a record in Australia and England Test matches.
- David Gower made his 3000th Test run against Australia.
- Wayne Larkins scored his highest Test score: 64.

Day one

England in charge, at last

GOOCH WON the toss in front of fifty thousand people and batted on a slow and placid pitch. Despite some wobbly moments, Gower and Stewart survived a testing afternoon to take England to stumps at 4-239 after both openers, Gooch and Atherton, had been dismissed with the score on 30. All in all, it was quite a good day for England.

Atherton, still looking out of his depth, propped too early onto the front foot in true county-cricket style only to be surprised by Reid's extra bounce. He was caught at short-leg by Boon for a duck. Gooch, horror of horrors, padded up to Alderman's off-cutter and was out leg-before to the Australian seamer for the seventh time in his career. It was Alderman's thirty-third leg-before against England and suggested strongly that the hoodoo he had held over Gooch was as strong as ever. As umpire Peter McConnell's finger rose and Gooch's glum shoulders drooped a little more, it looked like being a long, trying summer for poor England and its skipper.

Larkins battled away for three and a half hours, often playing and missing outside off-stump to the left-hander's angled deliveries, but rarely playing across the line for risky runs as he had in earlier games. That extra resolve took Larkins to 64 and kept the innings alive for Gower and Stewart to consolidate in the last session.

Larkins, a thirty-six-year-old journeyman from Northamptonshire, known to team-mates as Ned, was a surprise selection for this tour. A double century late in the county season against Gooch's Essex team sealed his spot. In county cricket the bushy-haired Larkins is a dasher; unorthodox but effective. In the first Test his tendency to plant his feet and hit across the line proved disastrous. But in Melbourne Larkins played much straighter, refusing to chase Reid and Alderman and always trying to drive straight down the ground.

Gower and Stewart followed Larkins's lead and countered Alderman's late movement by playing forcefully towards long-on and long-off. At last England was trying something in an attempt to negate Alderman. By stumps, that pair had addded 87, with a far more cautious Gower on 73 and a determined Stewart on 42.

Reid took two of the four wickets to fall and was by far the best of the Australians. Often he was too good, deceiving so easily that he missed the bat completely rather than finding the edge for a catch behind. That is why Reid was considered an unlucky bowler and had not yet taken five wickets in a Test innings. His time had to come.

It was not a spectacular day, both teams probing at each other, unwilling to go for the throat too early in the game. The wicket was slow for

IN PROFILE

Wayne Larkins

Born: 22.11.53

Tests: 13. Debut v. Australia, Melbourne, 1979-80.

Highest score: 64 v. Australia, Melbourne, 1990-91.

Nickname: Ned, after a character in a radio show called *The Archers.*

Favourite moment: Walking out to field in 1979 in the World Cup final at Lord's.

Horror moment: Getting a first ball duck in the same game.

Greatest influence: Mushtaq Mohammad, who was captain of Northamptonshire in the mid-1970s. His attitude and skills as a batsman were a great example.

Superstitions: Only one. I always like to walk out on the left side of my opening partner.

Favourite shot: The drive through extra cover off a fast bowler.

How do you overcome nerves? I usually have a cigarette.

Coaching tip: Simply, to watch the ball carefully and make sure you play straight.

both bowling and batting and accordingly Border placed most of his close catchers in front of the batsmen rather than in the customary slips. He knew that on this wicket he would have to be patient and prise England out.

On the second day, England's remaining batsmen would be looking to build towards a total of 400 to 450. Anything less on this slow strip would be a wasted opportunity.

DAY ONE: England 4-239 (Larkins 64, Gower 73 not out, Stewart 42 not out, Reid 2-71).

England's destroyer: Gooch's men could do nothing to counter Bruce Reid's bounce and difficult angle from leg to off.

A likely lad: Phil Tufnell relaxes during a net session.

Phil Tufnell: not just another English spinner

The English view

Alan Lee reveals the many reasons why Phil Tufnell became a cult figure.

MELBOURNE boasts the liveliest fish and chip shop in the world – a coarse, crazy barn of a café where the atmosphere challenges the most miserable man to have fun. Among the revellers present on Christmas Eve was Philip Clive Roderick Tufnell, whose jiving, interspersed with his specialty impression of Mick Jagger, so nearly stopped the show that all those who saw him will have followed the Boxing Day Test match with a new curiosity. Tufnell, the epitome of a Cockney wide-boy, was setting out on a Test match career which could establish a cult figure to rival Greg Matthews. It could also produce England's most attractive and effective spin bowling since the breed went out of fashion.

The alternative script is less endearing but difficult to discount. With Tufnell, there is always scope for the eccentric and the explosive. He is a total departure, and hopefully a refreshing one, from the automaton industry which some would have the England cricket team resemble; a rebellious spirit rampant beneath the carelessly-worn team uniform, the stubble and the smokes.

He is a determined Londoner, his speech doing away with initial 'h's and final 'g's in a way which hints he may be auditioning for a part as one of Arthur Daley's East-end associates in *Minder*. He has a streetwise face, cautious eyes and hair which has been cut short, to fashion, when, before he reluctantly reformed, it was worn pony-tail long – a statement which offended the conservative souls at Lord's beyond endurance.

Tufnell plays for Middlesex, whose base is the game's stately headquarters in St John's Wood. There have been times, he will confess, when the relationship has existed on quicksand and, two years ago, he was given an unequivocal final warning to smarten up his act or find another job. Being the character he is, Tufnell may have bridled at this, resented the imposition of being instructed to undergo a personality change when he was perfectly happy the way he was. It was a pivotal time in his life and if cricket can be grateful that he elected to conform, it should also applaud the way he has done so, for he may now respect conventions and expectations, but nobody could accuse him of entirely sanitising his persona. Ask the diners in The Last Aussie Fishcaf on Christmas Eve!

Tufnell's father was a silversmith in central London and, if crowded out by the conservatism of cricket, Phil may well have followed him into the trade. His schooldays had been a contradiction, for he started out at Highgate public school and ended up in the less privileged environs of Southgate comprehensive. He admits to being a bully, even to bowling his

Provocative poster: A few boys in the Melbourne Cricket Ground outer try to stir up the volatile Phil Tufnell.

seamers at the heads of smaller boys. But cricket, for a time, lost its appeal and it was only through being persuaded to go to the Middlesex indoor nets that he acquired the art of spin bowling and began to enjoy it.

He was twenty years of age when he made his debut for Middlesex and it was a fortuitous time to be emerging. The county had, for a decade, possessed the best spin pair in England in John Emburey and Phil Edmonds. Emburey's off-breaks and relentless chatter remain very much a part of the scene, but Edmonds, having failed to persuade the committee that he could mix cricket with his increasingly entrepreneurial financial work, retired in 1988, the very time when Tufnell was ready to step up in grade. Although, like Edmonds, he is a left-armer, Tufnell was never on the wavelength of his predecessor and quickly adopted Emburey as mentor. On this tour, they spoke regularly on the phone – Emburey's vast experience of Australia an obvious benefit. They are soulmate Cockneys, these two, but very different bowlers. Emburey's skill is frustrating batsmen out, but Tufnell attacks them with flight and change of pace. Angus Fraser believes him to be the most aggressive spinner he has seen.

One of the faithful: In his first Test, Phil Tufnell attracted jibes from the local crowd, but also delirious support from some hardy English fans.

His successful graduation to county cricket was followed quickly by jumping a considerable queue of similar bowlers to win his place on this tour. And, from the start, it was clear that he was capable of avoiding the traditional second-spinner blues. All too often, the perceived reserve player of two slow bowlers rapidly retreats to anonymity, sighted only when carrying the drinks, waiting for the team bus or bowling with ever-diminishing confidence in the nets.

This would not do for Tufnell, whose subdued and even surly veneer when first met disguises an inner confidence and an extravagant personality coiled for action. Known as 'Cat', though for his dressing-room sleeping habits rather than any special fielding qualities, he settled into a rhythm early on in the tour and quickly made it plain that here, at long last, was a man to displace the ageing Eddie Hemmings.

In the early World Series games, he was England's most consistent bowler. When a spinner was required in Melbourne, he was the obvious selection. And, in a gripping Test match far less one-sided than the margin would have one believe, he bowled perseveringly and proudly, deserving a reward which never came. Finally, sadly, it all got too much for him, and when umpire Peter McConnell declined to uphold an appeal for a catch behind against David Boon, in the Australian second innings, Tufnell lost control. By words and gestures he made his disgust too obvious. Graham Gooch had to intervene, McConnell had to be placated and the new boy privately reprimanded. His debut, after all, had ended closer to tears than triumph, but with Phil Tufnell, the game will always explore the full range of emotions.

Picking up the crumbs: Australian wicket-keeper Ian Healy caught every edge that Bruce Reid conjured from England's confused batsmen.

Day two

England crashes again

PATIENCE finally paid off for Australia and Reid on the second day as England lost its last six wickets for only 113 more runs and Reid broke the five-wicket barrier with career-best figures of 6-97.

As well, Gower made his seventeenth Test century and his first at the Melbourne Cricket Ground.

For most of the morning Gower looked eminently comfortable and the crowd of twenty thousand showed its affection with a warm ovation for his hundred. But, as befits such an enigmatic player, minutes later Gower spooned a simple caught and bowled back to Reid's long left arm and was out for the even hundred. 'Seventeen (Test centuries) sounds nice but a few more sounds even better,' Gower said later, indicating his desire to continue playing the only cricket that really challenges and interests him.

As for losing his wicket as soon as he had reached another milestone and earned the chance to take England towards a safe position, Gower recalled somewhat ruefully what his captain had told him that morning: 'He said that whatever I got would not be enough.'

Eventually England was all out for 352, failing to capitalise on the good work of the day before. And, worse still, Australia looked in ominous touch by stumps. At 1-109 with Taylor in easy control at 42 not out, the balance ended in Australia's favour. England had wasted another opportunity.

The MCG wicket had not helped the England batsmen play shots. With the bounce slow and uneven, they struggled to find a rhythm. Survival was relatively easy; scoring runs quite difficult. Yet on the first day, England's top order seemed to understand this. They occupied the crease and were prepared to build slowly towards a good total. On the second day Australia's bowlers showed more patience, rarely allowing free hits and forcing England's middle and lower orders to either fight patience with patience or take risks to accelerate the scoring. The Englishmen chose the latter course and so lost wickets too quickly.

Patience and self-control have always been features of English batting,

FOR THE RECORD – DAY TWO

- David Gower scored his eighth Test century against Australia and his first at the Melbourne Cricket Ground.
- Alec Stewart scored his highest Test score: 79.
- Bruce Reid registered his first bag of five wickets in an innings and his best Test match and Test innings bowling figures (6-97 and 7-51).
- Ian Healy took five dismissals in an innings for the first time.

but not so these days. If ever there was evidence that the traditions of English batsmanship had been forgotten by this generation, it came when three of the six England wickets to fall were caused by batsmen following Reid's sharp angle from leg to off. In 1989 Mike Whitney, New South Wales's left-arm bowler, was not selected to tour England because it was thought England's batsmen would not offer shots to his angle deliveries. How times have changed in English cricket.

Reid was superb and one sensed that now that the 'five wickets in an innings' barrier had been broken, he would go on to take over from the older Alderman as Australia's best bowler. 'A couple of times I've had four-for and had a chance for five wickets, and I've had a catch dropped,' Reid said. 'I thought the mocker was on me and I lost concentration there for a while. If that was a hurdle, I hope it's gone.' With Alderman and Reid unable to swing the ball, accuracy, angle and cut off the wicket were the available weapons. As Reid explained: 'It was just a matter of hanging in there, really concentrating on line and length and waiting for the batsmen to make a mistake.'

After two tight days it looked like patience and the ability to withstand pressure would win this match. Australia looked to have more of both.

DAY TWO: England 352 (Gower 100, Stewart 79. Reid 6-97). Australia 1-109 (Taylor 42 not out).

Career best: Bruce Reid heads for the dressing-room after finally breaking the 5-wickets-in-an-innings barrier with his 6-97.

Day three

The Jack and Angus Show

SO MUCH FOR Australia's patience. As they did in Brisbane in the first innings, on the third day of the Melbourne Test Australia's batsmen fell to loose and inappropriate shots, mainly cuts on a wicket of uneven bounce. At stumps England, surprisingly, held a 46-run lead.

Fraser did to the Australians exactly what Reid had done to the English the day before. And, like Reid, Fraser returned career-best figures, his 6-82 an excellent effort on a wicket that did not suit him. Like Reid, Fraser probed away over after over, forcing the batsmen to play every ball, testing their self-control.

In the first over of the day Fraser twisted an ankle and every England supporter must have feared that the long run of injuries had taken its worst turn: the team's best bowler lost when he was needed most. But Fraser is a thoroughbred and he shrugged off the mishap to lead a tight and impressive bowling attack.

Around the country bushfires raged. In Melbourne it was a sweltering day with gusty winds sending clusters of rubbish swirling around the

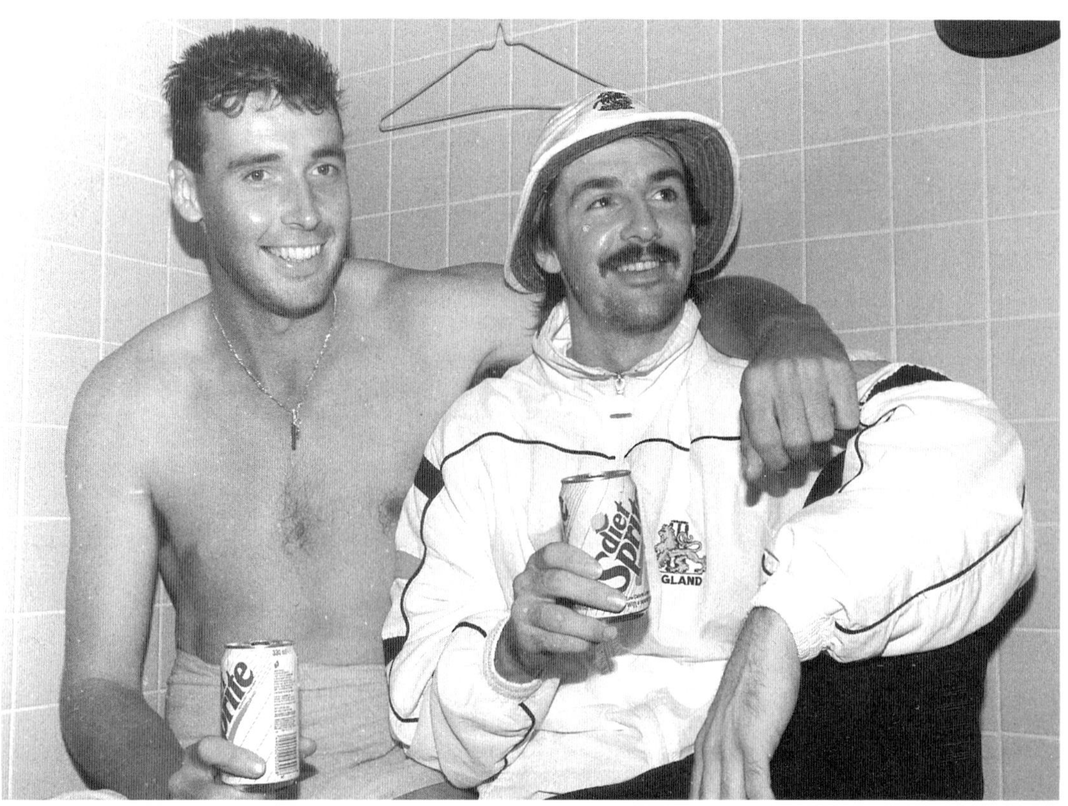

A pair of aces: Angus Fraser and Jack Russell pose for the photographer after their career-best efforts in Australia's first innings.

ground. On a day which tested tempers to the full, the long, loping Fraser bowled twenty-six overs for his 6-82. After play and a standing ovation from the crowd of twenty thousand Fraser, sore and limping, accompanied his small and chirpy wicket-keeper, Russell, to a press conference. 'I just tried to keep things simple,' Fraser said. 'On wickets like this, where there's no deviation off the seam, it's a matter of the bowler being more patient than the batsmen. The ankle wasn't a problem but I felt shattered by the end of a long spell. My legs were cramping up as I was running in to bowl but it's amazing what the prospect of a seven-wicket haul can do for you.'

From the moment he walked out at Edgbaston in the third Test of 1989 to bowl his first over in Test cricket, Fraser looked the goods. His philosophy is that of the traditional, miserly English seam bowler of whom he is a worthy successor. 'Bowling is basically about giving them nothing,' he says, 'keeping the pressure on the batsmen, making them work for every run. That's my philosophy. It's a question of patience.'

Coach Micky Stewart holds Fraser in high regard. 'He's the typical sort of English professional top-quality bowler that used to be about. He'll give nothing away. In the nets if he thinks someone has played one off an inside edge to fine leg for one he'll get miserable about it. He works like crazy.'

As Stewart suggested, Fraser is very good at looking miserable. His high, broad shoulders are forever drooping with a heavy work-load and the weight of expectations. But he also has a sharp intelligence and a fine, dry sense of humour.

Russell took six catches behind the stumps, equalling Rod Marsh's record for an Ashes Test and setting a new one for England keepers. 'No big deal,' said Russell from underneath the patched, sweat-stained floppy white hat he has worn since 1981 with a devotion bordering on the manic. 'The bowlers did the hard work and I just took the catches.'

True enough. Wicket-keepers cannot set catching records unless bowlers are good enough to get the ball to them via the edge of the bat. But it is also a great comfort for a bowler to know he has a keeper who will accept whatever chance a batsman is forced to offer. As a keeper, Russell had not done anything brilliant yet on this tour; but it was likely he would. He is all class – the latest in a long line of highly skilled, eccentric little English wicket-keepers.

When Russell accepted Ian Healy's edge off Fraser for his sixth catch and the record, the crowd gave both modest, courageous cricketers a fine ovation. The Melbourne crowd knows good cricketers when it sees them.

Malcolm, DeFreitas and Tufnell also gave Fraser good support. The usually wayward Malcolm seemed to respond to Gooch's leadership and looked much more the Test fast bowler, maintaining enthusiasm on a wicket that could well have discouraged him after a few fruitless overs.

This was the first time Australians had seen Gooch's ability to lift England out of the mire of 1989's Ashes defeat and the more recent traumas of this tour. All of a sudden, England was bowling to a plan, refusing to give Australia easy runs and looking much sharper in the field. On day

IN PROFILE

Jack Russell

Born: 15.8.63

Tests: 20. Debut v. Sri Lanka, Lord's, 1988.

Highest score: 128 not out v. Australia, Old Trafford, 1989.

Real name: Robert Charles Russell.

Favourite moment: My 128 not out against Australia at Old Trafford in 1989.

Horror moment: Being dropped from the England side this tour.

Greatest influence: Undoubtedly Allan Knott. I saw Rick McCosker caught Knott bowled Greig at Headingley in 1977, low down in front of first slip. I was thirteen then and that was the catch that made me want to be a wicket-keeper. I played against him a few times and now he's retired and doing some work for the Test and County Cricket Board. He's at every Test. He's like my personal coach, but I don't have to pay him. He's rung me half a dozen times on this tour. He was the greatest keeper ever.

Superstitions: Haven't got any! I try to make my equipment last as long as it can. That's probably one of the biggest ones. I'm very much a repetitive person. I like to do the same things day after day after day. I've got my hat. I've only ever played one first-class match without my hat. That was my first match. My keeping gloves are still with me. If I'm playing well I like to wear the same batting gloves, the same shirt, the same trousers. First slip gets wider and wider as the days goes on. But I like to keep the same gear even if I have to wash it myself overnight.

How do you overcome nerves? I wouldn't say I get nervous, I get excited. It's the same excitement I used to get waiting to play club cricket for my side back home every Saturday. I couldn't wait to play each week.

Coaching tip : A wicket-keeper should catch every ball. If you want to do it standing on your head, do it standing on your head. Wherever the ball goes, get it.

three England looked much better than the team that played a few weeks earlier in Brisbane, and Gooch's presence was universally considered the reason for the change.

Good captains are always seen to be in control and Gooch realises that. At one stage, he showed his appreciation for the dramatic niceties of the game when he stopped his team half-way out to the centre square, drew the players in to a tight circle and reminded them of what was needed for the last session, the session when many fielding teams lose the plot through weariness. This ploy began in the West Indies in early 1990 when Gooch was forced to hold his meetings on the field because of the paper-thin walls of the Caribbean dressing-rooms. Gooch persisted with this because he realised that calling his side together in front of the crowd and the opposition increased the impact of what he has to say.

Waiting, hoping: The door is closed, the wait is long, but the future is wide open for these lads waiting for heroes and autographs.

Some captains are born for the job, although not as often as England's traditional system of choosing its captain suggests – Eton, Oxford and all that. Others have the job thrust upon them, rely on their great skills as players to survive the early learning years and then mature into fine leaders. Border has done that and Gooch, a close friend and former team-mate at Essex, is doing the same. He might appear nondescript and only half awake under the broad Akubra hat he acquired for the hot Australian summer, but Gooch can obviously rouse not only himself but his players when the need arises.

For Australia, Taylor made a steady 61 but was restricted by England's clever tactic of bowling to him around the wicket and so cramping his usually fluent off-side play. With the ball coming into him from the off, Taylor has to be careful to choose the right ball to cut, one of his favourite shots. If the ball veers in too close he might not be left with any room to adjust to late movement.

Fraser got him like that in the first innings of the first Test, but Taylor showed his coolness by cutting well in the second innings. 'I'm not going to stop cutting just because I got out once to the shot, am I?' he said after the game. Nevertheless, England's bowlers did upset, albeit ever so slightly, the unhurried, remorseless run-scoring rhythm Taylor had established in each of his previous Tests.

With an average of 60-plus from those games, Taylor ranks among the greats. If he maintains that average, or near, throughout a long career he will sit second to Don Bradman on the list of all-time great Australian batsmen. A remarkable achievement on any terms; extraordinary for an opening batsman.

FOR THE RECORD – DAY THREE

- Jack Russell took six dismissals in Australia's first innings, a record number of dismissals for England in Tests against Australia.
- Steve Waugh made his 2000th run in Test cricket.
- Angus Fraser returned his best bowling figures (6-82) in a Test.

Dean Jones strode to the crease with all the swaggering purpose he usually saves for his one-day extravaganzas. Jones thrives on adrenalin and his slaughter of the England and New Zealand bowlers in the first section of the one-day series followed by his stunning hundred against England at Ballarat provided all the fuel he needed to fire him for a big innings in front of his adoring home crowd. With Border in a similar mood at the other end Jones attacked from the start, once more using his feet to take the game to spinner Tufnell. Jones made a brisk 44, added 75 in quick time with Border and became another batsman to fall to the wicket's uneven bounce when he cut at Fraser's first ball after the afternoon drinks break.

With those two on the attack Australia looked set to take control, but England fought back and it was left to Border to hold the innings together with a patient 62, an innings that ended up being more reminiscent of his back-to-the-wall efforts in the dark days of the early 1980s than the cameo innings he had played in the previous year or so.

Like the best Test matches, the game had been building slowly but inexorably towards a fascinating conclusion. After three tight and tense days, England led by 46 runs on the first innings. The question was whether the England batting could respond to the challenge of scoring enough runs in the second innings to put Australia under the hammer in the fourth innings on a wearing wicket.

Or would England squander its chance, as it had done in Brisbane when it also enjoyed the unexpected bonus of a first-innings lead?

DAY THREE: Australia 306 (Border 62, Taylor 61. Fraser 6-82).

Day four

Oh, England, how could you?

THE BUBBLE had to burst some time. After three tense days, the war of attrition this match had become broke out on the fourth afternoon in one of the most dramatic days ever seen at the MCG. In all, twelve wickets fell for 178 runs, with 8-31 in the last session.

England was bowled out for 150 in yet another second-innings collapse and Australia ended the day 2-28, with another 169 needed to win the game.

With his team enjoying a first innings lead of 46, Gooch would have aimed to score at least 250 in the second innings, giving England a lead of 300 and three sessions or slightly less in which to bowl Australia out on the fifth day. It was not to be.

This extraordinary day began calmly enough. Gooch and Larkins steered England to lunch at 1-42 and at tea things were still relatively sedate at 4-147. Larkins, continuing his good form of the first innings,

IN PROFILE

Phil DeFreitas

Born: 18.2.66

Tests: 20. Debut v. Australia, Brisbane, 1986-87.

Best Figures: 45 v. Australia, Adelaide, 1990-91. 5-53 v. New Zealand, Trent Bridge, 1990.

Nickname: Daffy.

Favourite moment: It has to be when I was first selected to play for England.

Horror moment: Losing the World Cup final to Australia in 1987.

Greatest influence: Ian Botham. On my first tour to Australia in 1986-87 he was a great help. Also David Gower, Allan Lamb and most of the senior players. At county level, Ken Higgs at Leicester and Geoff Arnold from Surrey.

Superstitions: None really.

Favourite shot/delivery: The cover drive; everyone loves a half-volley. In bowling, it has to be the away-swinger.

How do you overcome nerves? It's always good to have a few nerves. If not, there's something wrong. As soon as you get out there and get into it they disappear.

Coaching tip: Work hard at the game. Whatever you want to achieve, you can. It depends on how much you put into it.

IN PROFILE

Alec Stewart

Born: 8.4.63

Tests: 12. Debut v. West Indies, Kingston, 1989-90.

Highest score: 91 v. Australia, Sydney, 1990-91.

Nickname: Stu.

Favourite moment: Making my Test debut and then England winning the match. And I always wanted to play against Australia in Australia after spending so much time here.

Horror moment: Playing in a lot of losing semi-finals and never making a final. I've played in two losing semi-finals for Surrey, and for England in the Nehru Cup.

Greatest influence: I can't really say the Old Man can I? But certainly him, as a cricketer himself. Geoff Arnold at Surrey, and two Aussies during my eight seasons in Perth, Tony Mann and Kevin Gartrell.

Superstitions: I always put my left foot on to the field first, either to bat, field or keep.

Favourite shot: Anything that hits the middle of the bat really. Probably of any it would be the cover drive, but it depends on the bowler.

How do you overcome nerves? It's always good to be a bit nervous because it means you're hyped up. Nerves disappear once you get out there.

Coaching tip: The most important thing is to enjoy the game otherwise you won't play your best. And as a batsman, just to concentrate.

was on 53 and Alec Stewart on 8. Gooch had played superbly for 58 and it had taken Australia's best bowler, Reid, to dismiss him.

Until tea, England was cruising comfortably enough, the steady but relentless battle of wills that had characterised the first three days continuing unabated. In the middle session, after Reid dismissed Gooch and Smith, Gower was out for his first duck since August 1982. In between he had scored 5046 runs in 119 Test innings.

That wicket, falling to Matthews's persistent off-spin, kept Australia in the contest and the pressure on England. But Larkins and Stewart were playing sensibly. At one stage England went forty-three balls without scoring a run against Matthews and Steve Waugh. It was tense stuff as England ground towards a winning total.

Then the mayhem.

In the first fifty-one minutes of the final session the visitors lost 6-3 in twelve tension-packed overs, with Reid taking another career-best haul, this time 7-51 to give him match figures of 13-148. More of Reid later.

After tea, with Hughes suffering from a virus and Alderman denied his usual swing by a dry atmosphere and wicket surface, Reid and Matthews bowled magnificently, giving the Englishmen no free hits and testing their nerve to the limit.

In the end the Australians broke through; or rather the Englishmen cracked. Therein lies the difference between good and poor teams. The former play well when it matters most; the latter crumble when the pressure becomes too great.

Reid took an amazing 4-0 in nineteen balls and Matthews a relatively expensive 2-3. From the time Gooch was out, England lost 9-47 in the sort of collapse that denotes a team with a deep-seated sense of its own inadequacy.

Reid's match figures of 13-148 were the best on the MCG for eighty-nine years, the third best by an Australian on that ground and, apart from Bob Massie's remarkable 16-138 at Lord's in 1972, the best match figures by an Australian since the Second World War.

The quiet 27-year-old was a little non-plussed by it all after stumps. 'I was shown a list of the players who have done better than me and there were a couple of all-time greats on there and a few who aren't around anymore. I'm not really aware of what I've achieved. I just went out there with

FOR THE RECORD – DAY FOUR

- David Gower, in scoring a duck in the second innings, broke his run of 119 innings since registering his previous duck.
- Bruce Reid became the fourth Australian to take thirteen wickets in a Test at the Melbourne Cricket Ground.

13/77	MA Noble	1901-02
13/110	FR Spofforth	1878-79
13/148	BA Reid	1990-91
13/236	AA Mailey	1920-21

a plan to bowl line and length and I got wickets. Basically the pitch is about line and length.' Reid admitted he had never bowled better.

Although the Australians handled the pressure like a confident, mature team during England's innings, the tension told on them when it was their turn to bat late in the day. With ten runs on the board, Taylor and night-watchman Healy were out and a nervous Boon joined his old opening partner, Marsh, in a grim battle to survive until stumps.

Australia faced a long, nerve-jangling grind to reach 197 the next day against an England team that was now bowling much better than it was batting. Coolness of nerve would tell in the end. Australia, as expected of a team in better form for some time, looked the calmer on this fourth day. Anything was possible on the fifth and final day, but the match had so far been the sort of fluctuating drama in which, in the end, the better team was expected to prevail, however tortuous the process.

DAY FOUR: England 150 (Gooch 58, Larkins 54. Reid 7-51). Australia 2-28.

You beauty! David Boon is pretty pleased with yet another success for Bruce Reid. Graham Gooch is left to his own thoughts.

Day five

Happy birthday, mates

ON THE EVENING before the final day of the Melbourne Test, two old friends and former opening partners, David Boon and Geoff Marsh, celebrated their birthdays at a city restaurant. Boon turned thirty that day and Marsh would be thirty-two a couple of days later. It was then they decided it would be appropriate if they took Australia through to victory together.

Given the twists and turns the Melbourne Test match had provided during the first four dramatic days, this was an outrageous plan. Before play on the final day, Border had a quiet discussion with the two, reminding them that cross-bat shots like cuts, a favourite of both, and drives at wide balls, had brought about many dismissals in this match. It was wise advice and the pair followed it closely.

Boon and Marsh have been close mates since their teenage years when they toured England with an Australian youth team, and they bring out the best in each other. They often room together on tour and share an obvious affection for each other. Like most such duos, they are opposites in many ways: Boon the powerfully built shot-maker with a dry, mischievous sense of humour; Marsh the quiet, conscientious worker. Paired together in challenging circumstances they are worth more than the sum of their individual talents. And so it proved on the last day of the Test.

The old firm took Australia to the 197 required for victory in a cautious, measured, undefeated stand of 187 that was not without its worrying moments. Having added only one run to his overnight score of

IN PROFILE

David Boon

Born: 29.12.60

Tests: 49. Debut v. West Indies, Brisbane, 1984-85.

Highest score: 200 v. New Zealand, Perth, 1989-90.

Nickname: Daniel or Babs.

Favourite moment: There are two. Winning the World Cup and realising that I had hit the runs at Manchester that meant we had won the Ashes.

Horror moment: The morning after the day we won the Ashes.

Greatest influence: Jack Simmons, the Lancashire all-rounder who coached in Tasmania and later captained the state team. He coached me from age 10 to 18 and helped me a great deal.

Superstitions: I always put the left things on first – boots, pads, gloves.

Favourite shot: I don't really have a favourite shot. I try to play each ball as it comes and not look for the chance to play a certain shot.

How do you overcome nerves? I concentrate on deep breathing, pace the floor and don't talk to anyone.

What is the most memorable thing a fast bowler has ever said to you in the middle? In my first Test, Malcolm Marshall said: 'Boonie, are you going to get out or am I going to have to go around the wicket and kill you?' I didn't say anything back. I don't make comments to fast bowlers.

Coaching tip: Train hard and always set yourself goals. Listen to advice from everyone and then go away and use your own judgement about which advice to follow.

8, Boon survived a very close appeal for leg-before to a fast Devon Malcolm. Boon had been struggling for runs for some time and when he saw no movement from the umpire's arm he must have thought he had received a late birthday present.

After the traumas of the day before, Marsh and Boon played with respectful wariness. Knowing they had time on their side, they refused to take any risks as they gradually built towards the winning target.

The situation gave Boon the chance to build a good score and so fight his way out of a form slump. At times, the tension and frustration told on him and he tried to play the occasional ambitious attacking shot. At this, his mate at the other end would walk down and berate him, at one stage admonishing Boon by angrily clapping his right batting glove on his bat. 'Basically I was just trying to remind him of the few outs he's had in the last month and a bit,' Marsh said at an amusing press conference given by the two and their relieved captain after the game. 'Concentration's been the only thing that's been letting him down. He's been hitting the ball really well throughout it all.'

Border was delighted with the disciplined way his two senior batsmen gave him an eight-wicket victory. 'They were really desperate. These are two very hard-nosed cricketers. They've been through the hard times and even though he probably won't admit it, Boonie was under a little bit of pressure. It was a tremendous test of character and to win so emphatically was just icing on the cake.'

Boon would not say whether he had felt much pressure on his place in the team, but his relief was obvious at the press conference. The old sense of fun and mischief was back in public view again. As for being out there with Marsh, Boon noted drily: 'Batting with Swampy is great because we don't take offence at each other's comments.' Just as well, as there were more comments than usual during this partnership.

Despite the statistical ease of the eventual win, the day still had some tense moments. England's left-arm spinner Tufnell, desperately trying for his first Test wicket, was annoyed when umpire Peter McConnell refused an appeal for caught behind against Boon when the latter was on 73. It was a close thing and Tufnell, a youthful and more passionate player than most of his team-mates, attracted boos from the small but enthralled crowd when he kicked the ground at the end of the over.

Although it was Australia's day, the most memorable moment came in the middle session when Angus Fraser's sore hip finally forced him from the field. Fraser had not taken a wicket that day, but again had shown great courage and determination, not letting the pressure ease on Boon and Marsh despite his injury. As Fraser dragged his tired body from one

FOR THE RECORD – DAY FIVE

- Geoff Marsh and David Boon both surpassed 1000 Test runs against England.

side of the field across to the dressing-rooms, the entire crowd stood to applaud a talented and brave bowler. A wonderful moment.

At the end of play, Gower and Fraser walked straight into the Australian rooms to congratulate their opponents. By the time the umpires came off, Fraser had not emerged but Gower was standing at the door of the England rooms. As umpire McConnell walked past he handed Gower one of the match stumps. 'For Angus,' he said.

DAY FIVE: Australia 2-197 (Boon 94 not out, Marsh 79 not out).
RESULT: Australia won by 8 wickets
MAN OF THE MATCH: BA Reid (Australia)

The old firm: Geoff Marsh advises his long-time friend and batting partner David Boon as they cruise towards the winning runs.

Australia stands firm

IN THE FIRST Test in Brisbane Australia won only its third ever Test match by ten wickets after trailing on the first innings. In the second Test in Melbourne, it failed by two wickets to repeat that performance. Despite some anxious moments in both games, Australia's superiority was obvious.

In both games, the Australians rallied to dominate the decisive passages of play – as strong teams do. After the game, Geoff Marsh emphasised this point. 'The important thing was that we came from behind. We seemed to win the Tests in England fairly comfortably and we didn't have to work as hard as we did today. If we'd lost wickets early on we could have been in the manure.'

The Englishmen showed again that they were capable of matching the Australians for limited periods, but could not sustain the effort throughout the five searching days of a Test match. The kindest view of England's performance was that it showed it had enough talent to threaten Australia. Border, as generous in victory as ever, said as much: 'It's not going to take much for them to hit their straps. Gooch back as captain makes a hell of a difference and when they have Allan Lamb fit they will be working really hard to square the series.'

Something to smile about: Graham Gooch celebrates his OBE with a bottle of bubbly.

A less generous though more realistic view was that England's batsmen crumbled pathetically after their bowlers had worked to give them a chance of a win. It is not much use playing well for a few sessions and then falling apart so comprehensively. That is as sure a sign of weakness as any. Gooch admitted this: 'We lost the match when we lost 9-47 in the second innings and you have to put that down to bad batting. You can't explain it any other way. Games ebb and flow but if you are bowled out for 150 in any two-innings match you stand a good chance of losing.'

For Australia, Reid was outstanding and deserved the Man of the Match award. From the first two Tests he had eighteen wickets, a brilliant performance. 'Probably only Dennis Lillee in my time has bowled better,' Border said of Reid's form in this match.

Australian coach Bob Simpson confirmed what many observers suspected but found hard to believe: 'Bruce is definitely a better bowler now than before his back injury. He's got more life and this new action has somehow given him more bounce. I think he's got more pace consistently with less effort.'

Strangely there were some plusses to come out of the match for England. Fraser was magnificent. How guilty the England batsmen must have felt after they had wasted all his good work.

Devon Malcolm dispelled doubts about his temperament and Larkins about his ability to stay at the crease against a good Test attack. Gower's hundred proved his runs in Brisbane were not due to luck alone and debutant spinner Phil Tufnell showed enough spirit to suggest he would cause the Australians problems on the turning Sydney wicket in the next Test. And after falling meekly to Alderman in the first innings, Gooch looked ominous in the second. A big score by the captain was not far away although as he said when told of his New Year's honour, an OBE for services rendered on the deck of English cricket's sinking ship, 'I just wish I could have celebrated by leading England to victory in the Melbourne Test instead of to a defeat.'

Sadly for England, so many individual improvements could not distract attention from another poor team performance. The Australians again played as a purposeful unit rather than a collection of individuals, though with individual highlights such as Reid's hand of wickets and Boon's return to run-making. They were a formidable team and would have to lose some of their hunger for success if England were to have any hope of imposing its mark on this series.

Two from two: Allan Border whistles and claps his approval as Australia takes the second Test.

The Second Test
(Test no. 1160)

Australia v. England
Melbourne Cricket Ground
26, 27, 28, 29, 30 December 1990

Toss:
England

Twelfth men:
CG Rackemann (Australia);
CC Lewis (England)

Umpires:
AR Crafter;
PJ McConnell

Result:
Australia won by 8 wickets

Man of the Match:
BA Reid (Australia)

Attendance:
129,530

ENGLAND

FIRST INNINGS

Batsman	How Out	Ttl	Balls	Mins	4s	6s
GA Gooch (C)	lbw Alderman	20	33	29	2	-
MA Atherton	c Boon b Reid	0	11	15	-	-
W Larkins	c Healy b Reid	64	145	218	5	-
RA Smith	c Healy b Hughes	30	86	121	3	-
DI Gower	c & b Reid	100	170	254	8	-
AJ Stewart	c Healy b Reid	79	211	279	4	-
RC Russell (+)	c Healy b Hughes	15	55	69	1	-
PAJ DeFreitas	c Healy b Reid	3	5	5	-	-
ARC Fraser	c Jones b Alderman	24	55	69	3	-
DE Malcolm	c Taylor b Reid	6	19	32	1	-
PCR Tufnell	not out	0	9	13	-	-
SUNDRIES	0b, 2lb, 0w, 9nb	11	799	561	27	-
TOTAL		**352**				

FALL **12 30 109 152 274 303 307 324 344 352**

BOWLING

Bowler	Overs	Mdn	Runs	Wkts	NB	W
Alderman	30.4	7	86	2	2	-
Reid	39	8	97	6	1	-
Hughes	29	7	83	2	6	-
Matthews	27	8	65	-	-	-
Waugh	6	2	19	-	-	-
OVERS	**131.4**					

SECOND INNINGS

Batsman	How Out	Ttl	Balls	Mins	4s	6s
GA Gooch (C)	c Alderman b Reid	58	116	147	9	-
MA Atherton	c Healy b Reid	4	20	26	-	-
W Larkins	c Healy b Reid	54	171	232	6	-
RA Smith	c Taylor b Reid	8	15	14	1	-
DI Gower	c Border b Matthews	0	6	11	-	-
AJ Stewart	c Marsh b Reid	8	60	70	-	-
RC Russell (+)	c Jones b Matthews	1	33	46	-	-
PAJ DeFreitas	lbw Reid	0	4	3	-	-
ARC Fraser	c Taylor b Reid	0	6	8	-	-
DE Malcolm	lbw Matthews	1	14	21	-	-
PCR Tufnell	not out	0	0	1	-	-
SUNDRIES	7b, 3lb, 0w, 6nb	16	445	294	16	-
TOTAL		**150**				

FALL **17 103 115 122 147 148 148 148 150 150**

BOWLING

Bowler	Overs	Mdn	Runs	Wkts	NB	W
Alderman	10	2	19	-	4	-
Reid	22	12	51	7	1	-
Hughes	9	4	26	-	1	-
Matthews	25	9	40	3	-	-
Waugh	7	6	4	-	-	-
OVERS	**73**					

AUSTRALIA

FIRST INNINGS

Batsman	How Out	Ttl	Balls	Mins	4s	6s
GR Marsh	c Russell b DeFreitas	36	62	85	5	-
MA Taylor	c Russell b DeFreitas	61	177	256	4	-
DC Boon	c Russell b Malcolm	28	82	119	1	-
AR Border (C)	c Russell b Fraser	62	164	239	5	-
DM Jones	c Russell b Fraser	44	57	88	6	-
SR Waugh	b Fraser	19	47	61	2	-
GRJ Matthews	lbw Fraser	12	54	79	-	-
IA Healy (+)	c Russell b Fraser	5	10	21	-	-
MG Hughes	lbw Malcolm	4	15	46	-	-
TM Alderman	b Fraser	0	10	9	-	-
BA Reid	not out	3	16	16	-	-
SUNDRIES	4b, 12lb, 0w, 16nb	32	694	514	23	-
TOTAL		**306**				
FALL	**63 133 149 224 264 281 289 298 302 306**					

BOWLING

Bowler	Overs	Mdn	Runs	Wkts	NB	W
Malcolm	25.5	4	74	2	6	-
Fraser	39	10	82	6	9	-
Tufncll	21	5	62	-	1	-
DeFreitas	25	5	69	2	-	-
Atherton	2	1	3	-	-	-
OVERS	**112.5**					

SECOND INNINGS

Batsman	How Out	Ttl	Balls	Mins	4s	6s
MA Taylor	c Atherton b Malcolm	5	24	34	1	-
GR Marsh	not out	79	257	363	7	-
IA Healy (+)	c Atherton b Fraser	1	3	6	-	-
DC Boon	not out	94	234	321	8	-
SUNDRIES	4b, 12lb, 0w, 2 nb	18	518	363	16	-
TOTAL	**2 wkts for**	**197**				
FALL	**9 10**					

BOWLING

Bowler	Overs	Mdn	Runs	Wkts	NB	W
Malcolm	23	7	52	1	1	-
Fraser	20	4	33	1	-	-
Tufnell	24	12	36	-	1	-
DeFreitas	16	3	46	-	-	-
Atherton	3	-	14	-	-	-
OVERS	**86**					

Pure bliss: Australian captain, Allan Border, had plenty to laugh about after a draw in Sydney gave him cricket's greatest trophy in just three matches.

Sydney

THE THIRD TEST

4 – 8 JANUARY 1991

THE SYDNEY CRICKET Ground wicket, almost devoid of grass, slow in pace and generous in spin, is something of a disaster area for visiting teams.

A few years ago the SCG was the only venue where Australia could win. Its last loss there was against Mike Brearley's side in 1978-79 and leading up to this match Australia had won six Tests and drawn five.

The SCG has often been criticised, but more and more people are coming to understand that this wicket does two important things for Test cricket. Firstly it offers spinners more encouragement than most grounds have in recent years. This improves usually poor over rates, a blight on the modern game, and adds variety to the style of cricket played. Secondly the SCG has persistently produced dramatic matches.

As expected at such a venue, there was much speculation before the Test about possible changes to the sides. England made it plain that it thought two spinners a must. The choice of which pace bowler to drop was effectively made when England played its best bowler, Angus Fraser, in a one-day game despite the fact that the sore hip he had suffered in Melbourne had not fully recovered. Fraser was forced to withdraw from the Test – a devastating blow to England's hopes of staying in the contest for the Ashes.

Playing Fraser in the one-day match was an extraordinary decision. The England management said it saw no reason why the condition of his hip would be worsened by bowling ten overs in the game – a game England considered important in its fragile quest to qualify for the one-day finals. One really had to wonder at how this team was being run when its best bowler's fitness was sacrificed for the financial baubles of one-day cricket at the expense of the game's oldest, most revered contest, the Ashes.

Even *with* Fraser, England lost by 68 runs. As they did in the Melbourne Test, the batsmen collapsed pathetically, uninspired by Fraser's courage.

As well as losing their leading bowler, England was again to be without Allan Lamb. David Gower was to play despite lingering pain in the wrist he injured in Ballarat. Allan Border was typically sympathetic towards his friend and counterpart, Graham Gooch. 'It's a shame for him that he can't get his best side onto the paddock to mount the ultimate

Memo: England
From: John Major, PM
'Abstain from every indulgence ... take cold baths.'

Watching: Robin Smith with England coach Micky Stewart, in a familiar pose as the England team prepares for action.

IN PROFILE

Eddie Hemmings

Born: 20.2.49

Tests: 16. Debut v. Australia, Brisbane, 1982-83.

Best Figures: 95 v. Australia, Sydney, 1982-83. 6-58 v. New Zealand, Edgbaston, 1990.

Nickname: Eddie, short for Edward. The Whale, given to me by Ian Botham, apparently because of my alleged bulk. And Angus Fraser calls me Fossil. He says it has something to do with my age.

Favourite moment: Obviously your first cap for England. I took a wicket in my first over in Test cricket. Also hitting a four off the last ball to win the Benson and Hedges final at Lord's in 1989.

Horror moment: Not playing for England again from 1982 to 1987. And now, coming to Australia and being 41 instead of 21.

Greatest influence: Probably Clive Rice, as a captain at Nottinghamshire and as an example rather than as a coach. He always got the best out of me which was what I needed.

Superstitions: I try to keep away from them. I do lots of odd things but there's no pattern to them.

Favourite shot: It was nice bowling AB around his legs in the Sydney Test. Last summer I bowled a beauty to Mohammad Azharuddin. It pitched just outside off-stump, spun up the slope at Lord's, went through the gap between bat and pad and removed his leg stump. That's the sort of ball you want to be able to bowl.

How do you overcome nerves? I suffer unbelievably from nerves – always have. I'm nervous before I come on to bowl but once I get into it I feel all right. In county games, once I've been batting for a few overs and have got a few runs, I'm okay. But in Test cricket I'm always nervous when I'm batting, because I don't get many hits at that level and haven't got used to it yet.

Coaching tip: Never stop trying and work hard at your game.

challenge,' he said. 'I have sympathy for him because he's a mate of mine, but not for England in general.' It was difficult to argue with that.

Australia faced a dilemma in deciding its final eleven. With no decent leg-spinner to be found anywhere, Border was being pushed to take on the second spinner's role. But, as reluctant to bowl as ever, he was talking of keeping his options open by having a second specialist on standby. Peter Taylor bowled fairly well in the one-day game before the Test and was thought to be a chance for that second spot behind Greg Matthews. The selectors' view was that the variety of one good off-spinner and Border was better than the monotony of two off-spinners, one only occasionally up to Test class. The latter view prevailed and Australia's only choice came down to the familiar one of whether Merv Hughes or Carl Rackemann would accompany the drinks trolley.

Although the Fraser débâcle suggested otherwise, this game was do-or-die for England. A loss or a draw and the Ashes would be out of reach, retained by Australia in only three Tests. Even without Fraser, England's bowling was good enough to provide the Australian batsmen with another tight contest but, if its batting did not improve, the Ashes would be lost again as early as the half-way point of this third Test.

In a delightful aside, Britain's new Prime Minister, John Major, offered his own advice to Gooch. Mr Major suggested the England players '... abstain from every indulgence ...' and even take cold baths to try to transform the Ashes series. Given the lack of heart exhibited by some of England's batsmen in the first two Tests, cold baths might have been fatal.

Day one

Boon takes charge

EVEN BEFORE play in the third Test began, Australia struck a decisive blow when Border won the toss and grabbed the chance to bat first. In Sydney, more than at most grounds, the team that bats first can enjoy a huge advantage. Batting becomes more and more challenging as the days pass, the wicket wears and the spin increases; batting last can be daunting, especially for visiting teams unused to the conditions.

Batting on the slow Sydney Cricket Ground pitch requires a strange mixture of patience and aggression. Boon, something of an SCG specialist with three Test hundreds from his past three appearances there prior to this match, says batting at the SCG is as much a mental exercise as anything. 'I like the ground,' he says. 'It has a good atmosphere and that gives you a positive feeling about your game. You can play shots there. You can cut, you can drive, but you have to be more patient. You have to run hard between the wickets and make sure you hit the loose balls for four.'

Boon followed his own advice to the letter on the first day. Coming in at 1-21 and being joined by Border when MarkTaylor followed Marsh to the pavilion with the score on 38, Boon played a faultless innings of 97. Malcolm had responded very well to the challenge of carrying the England pace attack in the absence of Fraser and his early pace and aggression had accounted for both openers and put considerable pressure on the Australians. But Boon played a carefully constructed innings with exactly the correct mixture of watchful defence and decisive attack.

Mixed feelings: 'If you could get 90-odd every time you went out there, you'd be pretty happy,' David Boon said after his magnificent 97.

In the session between lunch and tea Border and Boon added 90 runs. Of these Boon made 60, 44 in boundaries. It was the sort of stop-start batting required in Sydney. With the wicket slow, Boon was prepared to defend against even reasonable deliveries and wait for short ones where he could use the slowness of the wicket to his advantage by moving onto the back foot and cutting with all his customary power. The pattern of Boon's scoring showed how well he took advantage of anything marginally loose. Unfortunately for England, its spinners, Tufnell and Hemmings, did not display as much patience as Boon and Border and often, trying too hard for spin and thus sacrificing length and direction, were hammered to the off-side boundaries.

When Boon reached the eighties, Gooch offered him three juicy deliveries which he dispatched with impressive power to move to 97 and one shot short of his fourth consecutive century at the SCG. When Gooch served up the widest and shortest ball of a poor over, Boon launched into a square cut only to hit it straight to Atherton in the gully.

As he reluctantly walked off, obviously annoyed with himself, Boon spat out a wad of chewing gum and hit it away with his bat in what has become a typical gesture from departing Australian batsmen. After play, he was philosophical: 'If you could get 90-odd every time you went out there you'd be pretty happy.' But he admitted to seeing the dollar signs as the century came in sight. 'I think I probably tried to hit it too hard,' Border said.

Border had been slower than Boon and fell 41 runs later when he swept at Hemmings and was bowled behind his legs by one that turned appreciably and surprisingly. His steady innings had steered Australia to 4-226 when he walked off 22 runs short of his twenty-fourth Test century. His twenty-third was scored in September 1988 at Faisalabad against Pakistan but, despite such a long gap between hundreds, Border's average had remained constant at about 52, a testament to his great consistency.

By stumps Australia was a comfortable 4-259 with both Jones and Waugh in the twenties. If the Australians could push close to another 150 on the second day, the match and the Ashes would be safe.

DAY ONE: Australia 4-259 (Boon 97, Border 78. Malcolm 2-58).

FOR THE RECORD – DAY ONE

- Allan Border made his 3000th Test run against England.

Border's battle to score his next Test century

ALLAN BORDER'S greatest asset as a batsman is the mental strength that has enabled him to perform consistently under pressure.

Early in his career Border made hundreds when his team most needed them. When he was given the captaincy he chose to lead from the front and as he continued to make hundreds he won even more respect from his team. But since September 1988 when he scored 113 not out against Pakistan at Faisalabad, Border has not been able to reach three figures in thirty-nine innings.

Why not? Border is thirty-five; not that old for a class batsman, but perhaps old enough to be suffering from a slight slowing of the reflexes. And perhaps that awesome ability to concentrate all his formidable physical and mental resources to perform under pressure has been dulled by the fact that Border at last has a successful batting line-up around him. No longer is he the only one, as he was in the early to mid-1980s, who can rescue the team from another collapse.

Border admits that he cannot command the range of shots he did as a young batsman. He no longer works the ball through the on-side for ones and twos like he used to. Consquently he has to wait and work more for his runs. 'I don't seem to be able to cut as well now,' he says. 'I've definitely gone off the boil a bit.' For some unknown reason Border, as open and honest as ever, says he has become somewhat tentative when batting. 'I know I'm not as positive as I used to be. I seem to have negative thoughts about my batting now and as a result I'm not as attacking as I used to be.'

Signature: AB are the initials, and the hands of Allan Border have taken this (and other) bats to the most runs by an Australian in test cricket.

After years of ups and downs in a demanding game, Border is always philosophical, although you can sense some controlled frustration at his recent run of 60s and 70s but no centuries. 'It has got to the stage where I definitely want to prove to myself that I am still a Test match batsman; that I am still good enough to score a Test hundred. I should know how to get a hundred; I've scored a few over the years. I'm still batting well and averaging well, but I'm finding freakish ways to get out.'

Border recalled that in the first innings in Sydney, a ground on which he never scored a Test hundred, he was dropped in the gully on 69. 'The single off the chance took me to 70 and I thought to myself: "Hello, this is the day I'll get that next hundred".' He was out eight runs later, bowled when he missed one of his favourite and best shots, the sweep.

What is fascinating though is that, despite his run of bad luck, Border's brilliant Test average of 52 has not been affected. There is no better evidence of his consistency and continued value to his team.

Never say never: Allan Border is batting as well as ever, his average remains unchanged at 52 – he just can't seem to crack 100 in a Test match. Border's run of 'outs' since his last century in September 1988, extended in Sydney.

Day two

England cold, Matthews hot

GREG MATTHEWS rubbed England's nose in the dry Sydney dirt on the second day of the third Test match. His near-faultless century, his fourth in Tests, on his beloved home ground emphasised Australia's depth and general superiority. Matthews, more a bowler than a batsman in this second phase of his international career, occupied the number seven spot. The six batsmen above him were rated the best top order in the world.

What England would have given for one batsman, in any spot, who could have played with the confidence and attacking assurance that Matthews brought to his innings. What England supplied instead was 'the worst day of the tour', according to coach Micky Stewart.

In the last session England's frustration produced some impetuous appeals and Hemmings was disciplined by team management for kicking the ball away in disgust after an unsuccessful appeal against Alderman. Television replays suggested the umpire was correct.

From the first over of the day the Australians showed they would take the initiative and push relentlessly towards a large total. Steve Waugh batted brilliantly to add 26 off 27 balls in the first half an hour and set the stage for his New South Wales team-mate, Greg Matthews, whose 128 came off 175 balls and helped Australia to 518 – too many for an England team that simply did not have the fight to recover nor, it appeared, the will to win. England's fielding was not so much amateurish or below par as disinterested – a far greater sin at Test level.

Although Matthews's innings was a copy-book attacking performance, there were those expected moments when he behaved with his usual idiosyncrasy. He had a problem with his batting gloves, made damp and slippery from excessive sweat caused by Sydney's notorious humidity. Matthews, who said he had apologised to Gooch for the delays, was forced to call twelfth man Hughes onto the field on numerous occasions for new gloves. Hughes's every entrance was greeted enthusiastically by the crowd, though less so by England. Eventually Hughes the prankster felt compelled to make a point and, in a nice touch, brought out a kit bag and spilled the contents on to the field.

When Matthews posted his hundred he thanked his wife for her support during what had been a tense return to Test cricket by carving her initials in the air with one of those sweat-soaked gloves. Later he said the source of his tension had been pressure he felt 'just doing my job in the side'. 'It's great to get runs but I have to take wickets,' he said. 'If I don't take wickets then I'm not going to hold my spot. I'd swap that hundred any day for four wickets in one innings of this match because that's my job.'

Greg Matthews is often treated as an eccentric and not much else. His true competitive character shone through in this match.

For someone often accused of being conceited, self-absorbed and loosely attached to reality, Matthews showed a clear if somewhat grim perception of his situation. He is eccentric and fiercely individualistic but, if you look closely and without prejudice, you will see one of the most determined, competitive cricketers in the game.

Devon Malcolm drew praise from Matthews for his brave display and deserved better than his 4-128 off forty-five wearying overs. Malcolm pounded and finally dismissed the dangerous Waugh and had Matthews caught behind off a no-ball on 68. He was superb. But apart from that and a brilliant leg-side stumping by Russell to dismiss Jones for 60 off Small's medium-fast bowling, the Englishmen looked and played like over-worked county hacks stumbling their way through another meaningless day at the office. And, as if to add insult to all those injuries, Alderman remained not out on the relatively Bradmanesque score of 26, his best in Test cricket.

After two days, Border had the score he wanted. As in England in 1989 he could attack as much as he liked in the field for the rest of the game, waiting for England's batsmen to capitulate yet again.

DAY TWO: Australia 518 (Matthews 128, Boon 97, Border 78, Jones 60. Malcolm 4-128, Hemmings 3-105). England 0-1.

FOR THE RECORD – DAY TWO

- Gladstone Small and Devon Malcolm both captured their fiftieth Test wickets.

Howzat: Ian Healy had a match to remember with dogged match-saving batting, a split eyebrow and a couple of catches.

IN PROFILE

Devon Malcolm

Born: 22.2.63

Tests: 16. Debut v. Australia, Trent Bridge, 1989.

Best bowling figures: 6-77 v. West Indies, Trinidad, 1989-90.

Nickname: For years at Derbyshire Geoff Miller used to call me Dude as in a 'cool dude'. Now it's just Devvie.

Favourite moment: In Trinidad in the West Indies in 1990 when I got my first ten wickets in a match. And I was happy getting Viv Richards out twice in Jamaica.

Horror moment: It's got to be right now, losing so badly to Australia.

Greatest influence: Our coach at Derbyshire, Phil Russell.

Superstitions: None really. I like reading my bible, but that's not a superstition.

Favourite delivery: Any ball that knocks the stumps over. Unfortunately at this level you have to bowl a lot of balls to do that.

How do you overcome nerves? It depends on the situation. Generally you have to concentrate, have faith in yourself, remind yourself that you've done it before and can do it again.

Coaching tip: Be prepared for lots of hard work. If you're a fast bowler you should concentrate on pace but don't get carried away with it. The higher you play, the more you find that pace is not enough. If you bowl fast but give top batsmen a bit of width they will hit you for four. And you must work on all aspects of your game, like batting and fielding.

Malcolm revisited: bold and brave

DEVON MALCOLM had made his point. He has a big heart, and a determination lacking in many of his team-mates.

Early in this tour Malcolm seemed uninterested in training, especially for less glamorous activities like fielding and batting. Watching him train, observers began to doubt the temperament of the West-Indian-born fast bowler. Did he have the wherewithal to make it as a Test fast bowler?

Malcolm answered those doubts in the Melbourne Test when he kept running in over after over on a wicket that would have quickly discouraged bowlers with less determination. Angus Fraser led the way in Melbourne but Malcolm gave him great support, maintaining pressure at the other end at crucial times.

In Brisbane, Malcolm seemed a little lost out in the middle, lacking rhythm and direction; but in Melbourne and especially in Sydney, off a longer, more rhythmical run-up, he seemed to respond to the urgings of his captain, Graham Gooch. It was a case of a captain knowing how to handle an important player and the player responding well.

With Fraser out of the Sydney Test, Malcolm had to carry most of the workload on the slow wicket. In the sort of tropical humidity that can drive players and spectators batty, Malcolm bowled with great control and effort throughout Australia's long first innings.

Malcolm is not without his faults. His fielding is too often sloppy and executed with poor technique, but that is partly the fault of county cricket which allows players to call themselves first class yet neglect an area of the game as important as fielding.

At the batting crease Malcolm is a delight. He has no defence and apparently one attacking shot, the cross-bat slog to cow-corner which rarely goes where it is intended. But he has fun when he is batting and watching him is a brief but enjoyable wait for the next surprise. And on more than one occasion he has actually withstood the bowling amazingly well.

England's much-vaunted recovery from the 1989 Ashes disaster had been a partial success at best, but at least Devon Malcolm played his part. On this tour he deserved more support.

Learning test: Devon Malcom started the tour slowly, disappointed in the Brisbane Test, but then became England's most reliable and powerful strike bowler.

Taking block

From the square

Mark Taylor relishes the challenge of Australia's varied wickets.

"ONE OF THE BEST things about playing a Test series in Australia is that all the wickets are different and challenge you in various ways. In England in 1989 all the wickets tended to be the same and players like Allan Border say this is often the case. In Australia the team that wins a series has proven itself the better side on all surfaces.

Brisbane usually bounces and seams around and pace bowlers are favoured much more than spinners. Batting is not impossible but you have to be careful of the sideways movement. Melbourne moves a little off the seam but is usually slow. The problem there is uneven bounce and, as we saw in the second Test, the bounce makes the cut shot very dangerous. In Melbourne you have to be prepared to work more for your runs, to play straight as much as possible.

In Adelaide the bounce and pace are almost perfectly consistent. Bowlers who pound the ball in get some bounce, and good spinners get some turn, but it is a great batting wicket, especially with short boundaries and a fast outfield. There it is a matter of getting your eye in early and making the most of the good batting conditions. Runs always come if you stay out there.

Perth is the fast bowlers wicket. It is faster and bouncier than anywhere I've played; probably more so than anywhere in the world. It can

IN PROFILE

Mike Atherton

Born: 28.3.68

Tests: 13. Debut v. Australia, Trent Bridge, 1989.

Highest score: 151 v. New Zealand, Trent Bridge, 1990.

Nickname: Athers. Boring really.

Favorite moment: My first trophy win for Lancashire at Lord's against Worcestershire last season. And then I suppose scoring my first Test hundred against India at my home ground, Old Trafford.

Horror moment: A second-ball duck in my first Test innings.

Greatest influence: My dad first and then all the boys at Lancashire, especially Gehan Mendis.

Superstitions: I put my left pad on first. I made my first nought in first-class cricket in a varsity match after having a curry the night before, so I never eat curry the night before a game.

Favourite shot: Anything that gets me runs really. I seem to be photographed a lot playing the back-foot cover drive so that is a special one.

How do you overcome nerves? I'm not a particularly nervous player. I get a few butterflies but nerves don't take over.

As someone spoken of as a future England captain, what have you learned from watching Graham Gooch on this tour? I have great admiration for Graham's desire to win. He gives one hundred per cent and he's a fair bloke. He takes a pretty dim view of players who don't perform up to scratch.

Coaching tip: Watch the ball. That's all.

move a lot on the first day when there is moisture in the pitch, but if you can survive the first session or so it can be beautiful to bat on. The thing there is to play the line of the ball. On slower wickets you might have to watch the ball on to the bat very carefully, but once the WACA wicket settles down, the pace brings it on to the bat nicely and you can hit through the ball much more comfortably than on other wickets. Because of that batsmen can often go on the attack and take bowlers apart.

My home wicket, the Sydney Cricket Ground, is often criticised by visiting teams. They say it is too slow and turns too much to produce good cricket. But, as Greg Matthews often says, the SCG has consistently produced great matches in the past few years, either Tests or Sheffield Shield finals.

The SCG wicket is slow and it does turn although the spin is usually consistent. That just means you have to be patient. It is not particularly hard to bat there and there are plenty of batsmen who have made lots of runs at the SCG. It is a psychological thing. Because the ball doesn't come onto the bat quickly, you have to wait for it. You also have to be prepared to play out maidens if the bowler is not giving you anything. That is why the West Indies don't bat very well here. They like the ball coming onto them so they can attack. When it holds up a little they still try to smash it and get themselves into trouble.

Because of the slow pace you have to try to put the bad balls away for four, to make the most of every chance to score runs. The only problem with that is that often the wicket holds up or the balls turn a lot and you can't always put a bad ball away. This is where England suffered in this Test. Eddie Hemmings, in particular, dropped the ball too short and the slow pace allowed Boon, Matthews and Border, all good cutters, to hit boundaries. If batsmen are hitting enough boundaries to keep the score ticking over they can afford to defend the good balls.

It would be a boring season if every wicket was exactly the same. Once you have played on each of Australia's Test wickets a few times, you know what to expect and how to adjust your footwork, shot-making and mental approach. It is a challenge to adjust to various wickets and that is what makes the game so interesting. ”

Day three

At last, England's day

Pick the star: There's only one man in the world with a bat like this – Graham Gooch, the England captain, scorer of a memorable 333 against India last year.

UNTIL THE THIRD DAY of the Sydney Test, Atherton's reputation as a traditionally patient, rock-solid English opening batsman seemed to be based on the same sort of suspect evidence as his team's alleged rejuvenation. Just as England had succumbed meekly in the first two Tests, so Atherton had plodded his way across the crease and fallen cheaply to bowlers who looked too good for him.

But on this third day, when another batting collapse would have forced England to follow on and face almost certain defeat, Atherton dug in with all the determination of the mythical British bulldog. He batted throughout the day for 94 not out, guiding England to 3-227 and a reasonably settled night's sleep.

Leaving the field at stumps with Atherton was Gower, undefeated on 33, having survived a confident appeal for leg-before in Steve Waugh's first over. Even England's staunchest supporters would only have whispered their hopes that England might have been moving towards a total that would put this game out of danger. Sadly for them, Australia's score of 518 all but ensured that England could not win. Despite Gower and Atherton's endeavours the Ashes would stay with Australia.

A young man with a smooth, pink complexion, Atherton has the pedigree of an English gentleman cricketer: he is a graduate of Cambridge and now plays for Lancashire. He captained the England under-19s and the Cambridge University team and not surprisingly has been touted as a future captain of England. At the rate those sad characters have been annointed then condemned in recent years, it might appear that any player has a chance of leading England at some stage, that it's more a matter of patience than suitability. Atherton has both and, it seems, a greater claim than most.

Before this innings the 22-year-old had made only 32 runs in four innings in the series and tales of his great batting in England in 1990 seemed to Australian ears to have been exaggerated already by the passage of time and a desperate national hope to see some decent England cricket at last. But on this day Atherton showed that not all the traditions of English batsmanship had been lost to shuffling feet and faint hearts. He does at least try to play straight and use his feet correctly.

As it happened, Atherton's turnaround in form was not achieved without a share of luck. He was dropped twice, on 56 by a diving Boon at short leg and on 85 by Taylor at slip. But good teams make their own luck and, although England is not yet a good team, its change of luck was no coincidence.

For application, this was England's best day with the bat so far. With Gooch, who made 59 and added 95 with his young opening partner,

G'day chum: David Gower, in very relaxed mode after play, exchanges one-liners with BBC commentator and journalist Christopher Martin-Jenkins.

Atherton showed the batsmen who followed that determination could reap some reward.

For Australia it was a frustrating day. Things did not go according to plan and Border was forced to switch his bowlers around time and again in the hope of unsettling Atherton's concentration. As in Melbourne, Alderman struggled on a dry, flat wicket and Rackemann battled away without extracting much bounce. Matthews had to supply most of the overs and he was always a challenge. But on a wicket that was still excellent for dogged batting, Atherton's watchful technique and mental discipline were enough to deny Matthews. In another day or so, as the wicket spun more, that might not be the case. Hence the great value of Atherton's effort so far.

Reid emphasised his skills by taking the only two wickets to fall to a bowler: Gooch and the struggling Smith, both caught behind by Healy. The other wicket to fall, that of Larkins, went to Border's deadly left arm which threw down the wicket with a direct hit from mid-wicket. Yes, such things happen in Test cricket as well as one-day games.

Towards the end of the day, Healy was hit by a ball from Matthews that bit, spun, and clipped Gower's pad before splitting him above the eyebrow. Healy, fortified with stitches, was back on the field in minutes, but not before Test cricket saw Mark Taylor keeping wickets. That may never happen again and in years to come may provide cricket trivia with one of its more obscure questions.

If Atherton could push on to 150 and Gower make another hundred, it looked like England might regain some valuable confidence. But no more than that. Any chance to stay in the quest for the Ashes had already been lost.

DAY THREE: England 3-227 (Atherton 94 not out, Gooch 59, Gower 33 not out. Reid 2-55).

FOR THE RECORD – DAY THREE

- Graham Gooch made his 6000th Test run.
- Mike Atherton recorded the slowest century in Tests between Australia and England.

MA Atherton	424 mins	England v. Australia, Sydney, 1990-91
DW Randall	411 mins	England v. Australia, Sydney, 1978-79
KJ Hughes	374 mins	Australia v. England, Brisbane, 1978-79

Trivial pursuit: Who kept wickets for Australia in the third Test in Sydney, January 1991? You're right: Ian Healy and Mark Taylor, pictured above, while Healy was off the field taking stitches into a wound above his eye.

Whack! An unfamiliar sight as Mike Atherton launches into the Australian bowling during his stonewalling century. Atherton held together the England innings, while making the slowest hundred in Ashes matches.

Day four

Balancing the scales

ANY DOUBTS ABOUT the value of Atherton's six-hour 94 on the previous day would surely have been dispelled as England built on its foundation to reach 8-469 by five o'clock on the evening of the fourth day. With less than an hour's play left, Gooch closed 49 runs behind and so began a last ditch attempt to bowl Australia out cheaply in the second innings and force an improbable England win.

By stumps Australia was 2-38 and England coach Micky Stewart was justified in saying: 'It's nice to finish, shall we say, on the attack.' The only worry for England was that the declaration, inventive as it was, might still have come too late to give England time to force a win. If so, some of the blame might be laid at the feet of Atherton and Gower for some rather slow batting.

Atherton took more than an hour in the morning to post what was the slowest Ashes Test century in history and the slowest at the Sydney Cricket Ground. He was again lucky, for replays showed he had been run out on 94. Early on he was hampered by a lack of strike, but once he

Happy? Sad? Don't believe the picture: This was just one moment of torment in an otherwise glorious century by David Gower, making it two in a row in Tests.

reached 100 England really needed him to push on to a big score and continue to rotate the strike with the in-form Gower who had begun the day with a blaze of strokes.

Gower, who admitted later that he had been quite tense overnight and before play started, began like a man without a care in the world. He took three fours off the first over of the day from Alderman and added 42 runs in the first hour to Atherton's one. But once he reached 80 Gower slowed down until he had made his century – his eighteenth in Tests. In his defence, he was probably thinking of England's propensity for batting collapses and the words Gooch had said to him in Melbourne: 'Whatever you get won't be enough.' During this period, too, Atherton was finally out and the new batsman, Stewart, took time to settle in.

If Gower had been told to chance his hand more and chase quicker runs, Gooch might have been able to declare earlier but with no larger a deficit. This would have given his bowlers more time to dismiss Australia and his batsmen more time to chase a winning fourth-innings target. Fanciful stuff ... but it may have been worth trying.

Of the Australian bowlers, Matthews sent down fifty-eight committed overs for a disappointing return of 1-145. For a man who admitted two days earlier that he could only secure his place in the Australian team with wickets rather than runs, it was quite an anti-climax after a fine 128 in front of his home crowd. Alderman and Rackemann both struggled, although the former picked up some relatively easy wickets late in the innings. Reid was still the best of the Australian bowlers but was forced off the field mid-way through the day with a callous on his right heel.

In the last session Malcolm made the most of the fifty-three minutes England had to bowl by charging in with impressive aggression. He dismissed Marsh with the score on 21 and when Hemmings was awarded a close leg-before decision against Taylor eight runs later, England had completed its best day of the series since bowling Australia out for 152 in the first Test.

So far the third Test had not been played at the helter-skelter pace of the first two. There had been no batting collapses nor brilliant wicket-taking. It had been more the sort of hard-fought, tight Test cricket that devotees love. But England no doubt left the ground at the end of the fourth day hoping that something dramatic would happen on the fifth and final day.

DAY FOUR: England 8 declared for 469 (Atherton 105, Gower 123, Stewart 91. Alderman 3-62, Reid 3-79). Australia 2-38 (Healy 9 not out, Boon 3 not out).

FOR THE RECORD – DAY FOUR

- Mark Taylor made his 1000th Test run against England.

IN PROFILE
David Gower

Born: 1.4.57

Tests: 114. Debut v. Pakistan, Edgbaston, 1978.

Highest score: 215 v. Australia, Birmingham, 1985.

Nickname: Lubo or Arctic Fox.

Favourite moment: Winning the Ashes as captain in 1985.

Horror moment: Losing the Ashes as captain in 1989.

Greatest influence: My friends and colleagues.

Superstitions: They are ever-changing: coloured socks are banned now.

Favourite shot: Back-foot through cover.

The worst tactic you have employed as captain: Declaring against the West Indies at Lord's in 1984 and losing by nine wickets.

What's the difference between a 0-4 captain and a 0-3 player? At least you don't have to explain everything to the press all the time, but it's still painful.

What has England learned from this tour? 1989 wasn't just a fluke for Australia!

A tip for captains: Relax and have confidence in your players.

Coaching tip: Watch the ball all the way.

If you weren't a brilliant cricketer, what other life would you like to have led? Aviator.

Day five

England, on points

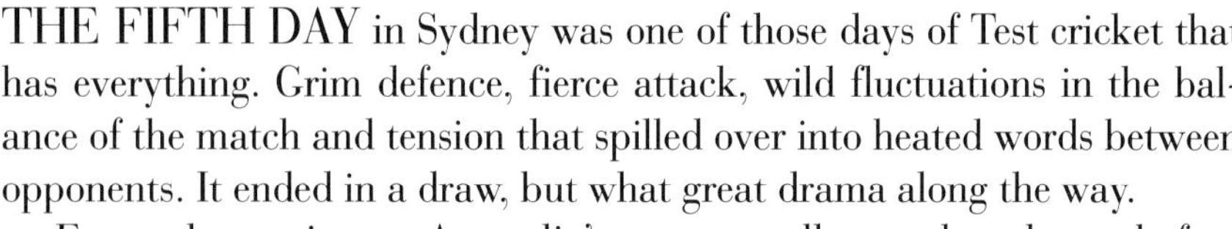

So close: Phil Tufnell almost achieved the ultimate hat trick: Border, Jones, Waugh. In the end a five-wicket haul was plenty of consolation.

THE FIFTH DAY in Sydney was one of those days of Test cricket that has everything. Grim defence, fierce attack, wild fluctuations in the balance of the match and tension that spilled over into heated words between opponents. It ended in a draw, but what great drama along the way.

For a change it was Australia's turn to collapse, though not before some back-to-the-wall defence against an England spin attack that smelled a whiff of victory and hunted it with a passion. Then in the final session, England's two senior players, Gooch and Gower, set about chasing 255 to win off a likely twenty-eight overs, a target of nine runs an over. It was a huge challenge and they made an impressive attempt.

Even before the innings of Gooch and Gower there had been heroics. Australia's nightwatchman, Healy, put up a fighting personal best of 69; Rackemann, a fast bowler with no pretensions to batsmanship, blocked the life out of the ball to stave off defeat and broke a record, for taking the longest time ever by an Australian to score his first run, set more than a hundred years ago; and Tufnell, in only his second Test, had a catch dropped that would have given him a brilliant hat-trick.

Would there ever have been a better Test hat-trick? When Gower dropped Steve Waugh in close, Tufnell missed a chance for a trio that would have read: Border, Jones, Waugh. Border was well caught by Gooch at square leg; Jones was caught and bowled when he left his crease to the first ball he faced, for no apparent reason other than his usual hyperactivity; and Waugh would have been out caught at bat-pad defending tentatively. 'A great way to play a hat-trick ball,' Waugh said with appropriate irony after he was finally out to Hemmings for 14.

Rackemann made nine in 107 concentrated minutes. He took 72 minutes and 75 balls to get off the mark, a feat that broke Billy Murdoch's Australian Test record set in 1882-83 and proved that cricket does not need continuous strokeplay to produce a great spectacle. 'I was batting for the Ashes,' Rackemann explained later.

When Malcolm, missing earlier from the attack because of back strain, was finally given the ball he immediately ended Rackemann's match-saving innings.

By tea England had bowled Australia out for 205. Tufnell had taken 5-61 and Hemmings 3-94 on a wicket that was now spinning sharply. Gooch and Gower came to the crease with great purpose, a buzz of expectation went around the ground, and within five overs Border had five men on the boundary. The two Englishmen were pounding balls to all parts of the field with orthodox but brilliant shots. They put 50 on the board in thirty-five minutes and added 84 for the first wicket. Gooch, in particular, was awesome in his power and positive intent. He is a captain who knows the best way to lead is by example and his 54 from 42 balls was a valiant if ultimately unsuccessful gesture.

Realistically England had little hope of sustaining such a pace and eventually lost four wickets for sixteen runs and its last small hope of staying in the quest for the Ashes. Had England chased those quicker runs the day before, it might well have had enough time on the last afternoon to reach the winning target. But wisdom after the event is always easy.

'Today wasn't our greatest day and we had to struggle to save it,' Border conceded. 'It's more of a relief getting out of the game than any ecstasy but, as someone said, we've done it (retained the Ashes) in three Tests which is pretty impressive.'

For the Englishmen, a series win was now impossible but, in between a few ordinary sessions in the field, they had shown plenty of fight. Unfortunately it had come too late.

DAY FIVE: Australia 205 (Healy 69. Tufnell 5-61, Hemmings 3-94, Malcolm 2-19). England 4-113 (Gooch 54, Gower 36. Matthews 2-26).
RESULT: Match drawn
MAN OF THE MATCH: MA Atherton (England)

IN PROFILE

Carl Rackemann

Born: 3.6.60

Tests: 12. Test Debut v. England, Brisbane, 1982-83.

Best figures: 6-86 v. Pakistan, Perth, 1983-84.

Nickname: Mocca, because when I first started playing for Queensland I used to wear a pair of moccasins.

Favourite moment: Being chosen for my first Test on my home ground against England.

Horror moment: Not winning the Sheffield Shield final in Sydney in 1984-85. I bowled a lot of overs and we came very close, but New South Wales just got up.

Greatest influence: No one in particular. There have been a few people along the way, but no one special person.

Superstitions: Plenty. The main one is not leaving your seat in the dressing-room during a good partnership. There are others, but none unusual enough to warrant mentioning.

Favourite delivery: One that gets a wicket. I don't care what it is as long as it gets someone out.

How do you overcome nerves? They have never been a problem. I'm just not a nervous person.

Coaching tip: Once you've achieved accuracy, don't sacrifice it for everything else.

FOR THE RECORD – DAY FIVE

- David Gower made his 8000th Test run.
- Carl Rackemann took 72 minutes to register his first run in Australia's second innings, the slowest score by an Australian in Test cricket.

CG Rackemann	72 mins	against England, Sydney, 1990-91
WL Murdoch	70 mins	against England, Sydney, 1882-83
RM Hogg	69 mins	against West Indies, Adelaide, 1984-85

So near, so far: David Boon leaves the field after his marvellous 97 in the Australian first innings. The swish of the bat is for the well-used chewing gum, on its way into oblivion.

Australia's Ashes

ENGLAND'S EFFORT in comfortably drawing the third Test was a vast improvement on its previous performances, but ultimately it was as futile as Gooch and Gower's great batting on that last afternoon. With two Tests to go, pride was all that England could regain. The Ashes were already safe in Australian hands.

Making 8-469 in the first innings when chasing 518 was a morale-boosting effort from England's previously fragile batting line-up but, for once, England's bowling let Gooch down. In combination with sloppy fielding and Australia's positive batting, England's short and wide bowling cost it any chance of winning the game and staying in the series.

For Australia, there were some worries at the top of the batting order, with Marsh and Taylor both falling to Malcolm, a bowler similar to those they would face in the West Indies in a matter of weeks. In the first innings it was Australia's depth of batting that saw it through those early setbacks. Boon at number three made 97, then Border 78, Jones 60, Waugh 48, the all-rounder Matthews 128 and Healy at number eight a useful 35. England, in contrast, was never able to rely on such a long list of batting contributors and again found it difficult to recover from the loss of early wickets.

In the third Test it was basically a case of one team being better than the other: better balanced, better prepared, better in temperament and, when one recalled Fraser's selection in that one-day game which ensured he would not be fit for the Test, better managed. Australia's batsmen were experienced, talented and match-hardened. England's were injury-prone, out of form or suspect at this level.

At his post-match press conference Border's mind was already looking past the rest of this one-sided series to the greater challenge his team would face on its forthcoming tour of the West Indies. If this indicated the Australians might succumb to complacency, the selectors had the opportunity to change some personnel, to remind the team that there were some gifted players awaiting their turn in Test cricket. Queensland fast-bowler Craig McDermott had a chance to impress against England in the tour match on the Gold Coast the following weekend; and Mark Waugh had already done all he could to push his claims.

Gooch's mind was stuck very much on present problems: how to improve England's batting, fielding and ability to play good cricket session after session, day after day. Lamb would almost certainly be back for the fourth Test in Adelaide, but would Fraser be ready to resume his place as England's leading bowler? If Fraser did not play in the fourth Test, England would struggle to dismiss Australia on Adelaide's beautiful batting wicket.

**Border's mind was already looking past the rest of this one-sided series ...
Gooch's mind was stuck very much on present problems.**

The Third Test
(Test no. 1161)

Australia v. England
Sydney Cricket Ground
4, 5, 6, 7, 8 January 1991

Toss:
Australia

Twelfth men:
MG Hughes (Australia);
PAJ DeFreitas (England)

Umpires:
AR Crafter;
PJ McConnell

Result:
Drawn

Man of the Match:
MA Atherton (England)

Attendance:
106,304

AUSTRALIA

FIRST INNINGS

Batsman	How Out	Ttl	Balls	Mins	4s	6s
GR Marsh	c Larkins b Malcolm	13	41	55	2	–
MA Taylor	c Russell b Malcolm	11	47	79	2	–
DC Boon	c Atherton b Gooch	97	174	201	17	–
AR Border (C)	b Hemmings	78	184	251	10	–
DM Jones	st Russell b Small	60	120	200	7	–
SR Waugh	c Stewart b Malcolm	48	61	66	8	–
GRJ Matthews	c Hemmings b Tufnell	128	175	242	17	–
IA Healy (+)	c Small b Hemmings	35	61	93	2	–
CG Rackemann	b Hemmings	1	8	15	–	–
TM Alderman	not out	26	73	86	1	–
BA Reid	c Smith b Malcolm	0	7	15	–	–
SUNDRIES	5b, 8lb, 0w, 8nb	21	951	657	66	–
TOTAL		**518**				
FALL	**21 38 185 226 292 347 442 457 512 518**					

BOWLING

Bowler	Overs	Mdn	Runs	Wkts	NB	W
Malcolm	45	12	128	4	7	–
Small	31	5	103	1	1	–
Hemmings	32	7	105	3	–	–
Tufnell	30	6	95	1	–	–
Gooch	14	3	46	1	–	–
Atherton	5	–	28	–	–	–
OVERS	**157**					

SECOND INNINGS

Batsman	How Out	Ttl	Balls	Mins	4s	6s
MA Taylor	lbw Hemmings	19	31	39	2	–
GR Marsh	c Stewart b Malcolm	4	13	26	–	–
IA Healy (+)	c Smith b Tufnell	69	160	165	6	–
DC Boon	c Gooch b Tufnell	29	72	73	3	–
AR Border (C)	c Gooch b Tufnell	20	29	34	3	–
DM Jones	c & b Tufnell	0	1	1	–	–
SR Waugh	c Russell b Hemmings	14	28	32	2	–
GRJ Matthews	b Hemmings	19	56	72	–	–
CG Rackemann	b Malcolm	9	102	107	–	–
TM Alderman	c Gower b Tufnell	1	10	10	–	–
BA Reid	not out	5	32	28	–	–
SUNDRIES	0b, 16lb, 0w, 0nb	16	534	300	16	–
TOTAL		**205**				
FALL	**21 29 81 129 129 166 166 189 192 205**					

BOWLING

Bowler	Overs	Mdn	Runs	Wkts	NB	W
Malcolm	6	1	19	2	–	–
Small	2	1	6	–	–	–
Hemmings	41	9	94	3	–	–
Tufnell	37	18	61	5	–	–
Atherton	3	1	9	–	–	–
OVERS	**89**					

ENGLAND

FIRST INNINGS

Batsman	How Out	Ttl	Balls	Mins	4s	6s
GA Gooch (C)	c Healy b Reid	59	127	148	5	–
MA Atherton	c Boon b Matthews	105	349	451	8	–
W Larkins	run out	11	33	44	2	–
RA Smith	c Healy b Reid	18	50	67	3	–
DI Gower	c Marsh b Reid	123	236	312	15	–
AJ Stewart	lbw Alderman	91	146	157	12	–
RC Russell (+)	not out	30	64	90	3	–
GC Small	lbw Alderman	10	21	28	1	–
EE Hemmings	b Alderman	0	3	2	–	–
PCR Tufnell	not out	5	15	22	1	–
SUNDRIES	1b, 8lb, 0w, 8nb	17	1044	665	50	–
TOTAL	**8 wickets declared for**	**469**				
FALL	**95 116 156 295 394 426 444 444**					

BOWLING

Bowler	Overs	Mdn	Runs	Wkts	NB	W
Alderman	20.1	4	62	3	2	–
Reid	35.1	9	79	3	4	–
Rackemann	25.5	5	89	–	–	–
Matthews	58	16	145	1	2	–
Border	19	5	45	–	–	–
Waugh	14	3	40	–	–	–
OVERS	**172.1**					

SECOND INNINGS

Batsman	How Out	Ttl	Balls	Mins	4s	6s
GA Gooch (C)	c Border b Matthews	54	42	68	7	–
DI Gower	c Taylor b Matthews	36	38	53	3	–
W Larkins	lbw Border	0	3	2	–	–
AJ Stewart	run out	7	10	10	–	–
RA Smith	not out	10	27	31	1	–
MA Atherton	not out	3	32	28	–	–
SUNDRIES	0b, 1lb, 0w, 2nb	3	152	100	11	–
TOTAL	**4 wickets for**	**113**				
FALL	**84 84 100 100**					

BOWLING

Bowler	Overs	Mdn	Runs	Wkts	NB	W
Alderman	4	–	29	–	2	–
Rackemann	3	–	20	–	–	–
Matthews	9	2	26	2	–	–
Border	9	1	37	1	–	–
OVERS	**25**					

Schoolboy cricket

The English view
Alan Lee

'What we have here ... are men incapable of top-class fielding through being aged, infirm and uncoordinated.'

EVERY TEST MATCH has its snapshot memories. The third Test in Sydney provided a bigger, brighter collection than usual. My personal album would include Jack Russell's stunning leg-side stumping off Gladstone Small; Greg Matthews's emotion on making his fourth Test hundred; David Gower's vivid strokeplay; Philip Tufnell's justified animation and Eddie Hemmings's unjustified petulance. And one more snapshot, perhaps the most memorable of all, is of Graham Gooch's contorted features as he watched the worst fielding he can ever have experienced as an England player.

Saturday afternoon at the Sydney Cricket Ground was a session which will live with Gooch an uncomfortable time for its utter awfulness. It was the session that cost England its best chance of victory; in essence, it cost it any interest in regaining the Ashes. And, let it be clear, there were no mitigating circumstances, no ill fortune, not even any especially formidable opposition. England simply played schoolboy cricket in a pivotal session of a decisive Test match. Gooch's face, even under the wide-brimmed sun-hat and behind the dark stubble, expressively captured the mood of horror.

The fateful session began with England's desultory outfielders showing a notable facility for turning ones into twos and twos into threes. It developed with some misfields which would have been funny had they not been so costly, allied to bowling which, Devon Malcolm heroically apart, would have done no justice to a village team. It ended with a properly rejected appeal provoking a juvenile tantrum from a man just short of his forty-second birthday. For the soccer equivalent of kicking the ball violently against the stumps, and in alarming proximity to the disobliging umpire, Hemmings would have had at least a yellow card waved in his furious face. Instead, he received a sharp, gesturing rebuke from Gooch in public and, perhaps, a fine in private.

Foolishly immature though it was, Hemmings's behaviour was symptomatic of the frustration boiling over within every England player as the game slipped away, or apparently so, through their own inadequacies. Back in the balconied dressing-rooms within Sydney's ancient and dignified pavilion, Micky Stewart must have wished he could once more take to his bed. England's coach had been through a rough time, first with a chest infection and then with a numbing virus. On-field events certainly did not aid his recovery rate and only in Sydney had he felt well enough to resume his most public duties – organising the fielding practice.

Stewart's strutting figure, cap on head as he either flicks and nicks endless catches to a notional slip formation or thrashes skyers into the deep-field with a sergeant-majorish bark of the intended catcher's nickname, has been one of the few unchanging sights of England cricket in the past four years. Captains have come and gone at a confusing rate, players have passed through as much as thirty per series, but Micky's beloved fielding routines proceed on a daily basis. There are those, myself included, who have frequently wondered whether a disproportionate amount of time has been spent on this, for little discernible return. Perhaps even Stewart now feels the same?

Certainly, Gooch's words at the end of a Test in which he personally could have done precious little more to inspire and motivate, did not quite ring true. 'Our fielding was way below standard,' he said, 'and we must work harder on it.' No, Graham, this time work will not be sufficient. What we have here, within a team which can otherwise lift its game in most areas, are men incapable of top-class fielding through being aged, infirm and uncoordinated.

Even David Gower's speed over the ground, possibly unmatched on either side, was rendered redundant by his inability to throw without wrenching his shoulder or aggravating his wrist. Gooch and Lamb are sound fielders increasingly compromised by injuries; Alec Stewart stands out, Smith just below him; most of the rest are careless, clumsy, cumbersome or some combination.

Time was when England's ground-fielding was its pride and joy. In the painful evidence of an otherwise riveting Sydney Test, those days will not return until there is another change of shift in the side; only then will Micky's fielding routines cease to appear somewhat futile.

Woe is me: On the field Graham Gooch watched the worst fielding he had ever seen. Off the field he could but think of ways to remedy it. In Sydney, apparently, he could think of nothing.

Congratulations: Mark Waugh acknowledges the applause of the crowd after achieving every young boy's dream – a century in his first Test. Waugh came to the wicket at 4-104 and took Australia to safe territory.

Adelaide

THE FOURTH TEST

25 – 29 JANUARY 1991

All eyes were on the gifted and elegant debutant, Mark Waugh.

TO BIGGLE or not to biggle seemed to be the burning question in the days leading to the fourth Test in Adelaide. David Gower and John Morris's stunt in joy-riding over the Carrara ground on Queensland's Gold Coast, as a salute to Robin Smith's long-awaited return to form, at least brought some comic relief to what had been another disaster-prone few weeks for England between the third and fourth Tests.

Two days after the Sydney draw, England flew to Melbourne to try to win its remaining one-day game against the Australians. In front of fifty-six thousand people the Englishmen fell three runs short and so suffered the indignity of missing the finals.

A match against New South Wales was hastily arranged, to be played in the large country town of Albury. While Australia thrashed New Zealand 2-0 in the one-day finals, in the bush England lost by six wickets to New South Wales, the reigning Sheffield Shield champions. New South Wales was without its three international players, the Waugh twins and Mark Taylor, and though the team did have plenty of depth, England's effort was again very poor, with only Mike Atherton carrying the flag with a fine second-innings century.

After the game Geoff Lawson, New South Wales captain, said of the England team: 'It's tough to come up-country and play an unscheduled game, but you really have to play with more discipline than they did. You have to have a lot of pride in every game you play.' Enough said.

From there it was on to the Gold Coast and its lurid delights. Playing on a converted Australian Rules football field, England finally broke the long drought. The Border-less Queenslanders, most of whom seemed lulled into complacency by the carnival atmosphere, allowed England to avoid having the worst win-loss record of any Ashes team visiting these fatal shores.

Smith and Morris both made hundreds; Gooch 93. Queensland's Stuart Law made a fine 73 and out-shone England's soon-to-be great white hope, Zimbabwian-born Graeme Hick, who managed to boost his Shield average with a score of 45. To rub it in a little, Ian Healy and Craig McDermott made half-centuries in the first innings before England bowled Queensland out a second time for only 175.

Fun and games: England's management did not see the funny side of David Gower's flight over Carrara, but the fans certainly did.

What ho, old chap: Cheery grins from David Gower and John Morris as they return to terra firma aboard a trusty old Tiger Moth. The pair's buzz over the Carrara ground cost them one thousand pounds each, enough for a return trip to London, if you shop around.

The amazing Tiger Moth fly-past, by Group Captain Gower and Flight Lieutenant Morris, took place on the third day. During the flight one of the touring English photographers realised that there were England players in the planes, and a completely unaware team manager, Peter Lush, was asked about the episode immediately after play. 'I know nothing about it,' he said. 'Biggles and Bertie' had apparently ducked out of the ground without permission and Lush was embarrassed and unimpressed. 'I'll investigate it,' he said. 'Of course, I wouldn't have approved it.'

Gower's comments were as entertaining as ever. 'It was a nice day for flying. I was very relaxed, flying by the seat of my pants. It was a literal buzz.' It was revealed later that the pair had planned to water-bomb the ground, but had eventually thought better of the idea.

While the management dithered about what action to take, England cruised to a ten-wicket win. Gooch, however, was not impressed with this long-awaited first-class victory. 'Our general cricket has got to improve. It's not been up to the standard required at international level, I'm afraid. Just because you've won one game doesn't mean it's all right. People have got to double their efforts and if they don't, well, it's their careers.'

The next day Lush announced that the joy-riders had been fined one thousand pounds each, the maximum available penalty. Lush's official statement read in part: 'While appreciating the incident was meant to be no more than a prank, management considered it to be immature, ill-judged and ill-timed. I am also very disappointed that Gower and Morris agreed that photographs for publication in newspapers could be taken when they landed and also at the end of play.'

Gower expressed no regrets. 'It was too good an opportunity to miss,' he said. But he did express relief that the episode was over so he could concentrate on the forthcoming Adelaide Test. 'I think Peter used the word "ill-judged" and he might have a point.' As for the severity of the fine, Gower's whimsical sense of humour broke free again. 'I'm not ecstatic about paying a thousand pounds for twenty minutes in the air. It's more than commercial rates and, in these times of deregulation, it's a scandal.'

The one piece of news in this period that rivalled the 'Biggles and Bertie' affair was the announcement that Steve Waugh had been replaced in the Australian Test team by his twin brother Mark. Steve, forced to carry the full load of a Test career from twenty years of age, had finally succumbed to the prolonged pressure. Over time, a few technical deficiencies had been exploited more and more by the world's best bowlers. In his place came his brother, who had waited in the wings for so long – one hundred first-class games in fact – gradually developing the grit and determination to score heavily for months on end. No one could have done more to warrant selection than Mark, with twenty-five centuries in those one hundred matches.

The one piece of news in this period that rivalled the 'Biggles and Bertie' affair was the announcement that Steve Waugh had been replaced in the Australian team by his twin brother Mark.

Mark was told the news by his brother. 'Congratulations, you're in the Test side,' Steve had said when they met at their parents' Sydney home. 'Thanks,' replied Mark. 'Who's been dropped?' 'I have,' said Steve to silence.

So, finally, to Adelaide where the past five Tests had ended in draws. England decided that on this great batting wicket it would need five bowlers, especially as Angus Fraser had played only a single one-day game since New Year's Day and was still below full fitness. Making room for the extra bowler, Jack Russell, whom many consider the best wicket-keeper in the world, was dropped from the side in a tragic turn of events. Alec Stewart was to keep for the first time in a Test and bat at number six, fulfilling the all-rounder's role in an unusual way. It was likely Phil DeFreitas would be the fifth bowler, having arrived as an emergency just before the Sydney Test.

Australia was to rest Terry Alderman, whose groin strain was still troubling him. Allan Border was suffering the same problem but would play regardless. And, as well as the in-form Mark Waugh, Craig McDermott had forced his way in, at the expense of Carl Rackemann. By these decisions, the Australian selectors showed that they were prepared to use some of the undoubted talent around the country in their efforts to field the strongest possible team – two Tests to nil or not.

This was the first Test in which Gooch and Lamb were to take the field together. Would it be a turning point? Probably not. Despite the extra bowler, it was hard to foresee England bowling Australia out twice to win the game.

Of more interest was the possibility that this match might produce a memorable start to another fine Test career. All eyes were on the gifted and elegant debutant, Mark Waugh, or 'Junior' as he has come to be known in cricket circles. There is always an extra buzz at a ground when a talented player is about to make his Test debut: are we going to be lucky enough to see cricket history being made? If Ladbrokes had been laying odds on a debut Test century from Waugh, it would have been a tempting bet.

Gooch breaks the news: Fraser in, Russell out

The English view

Alan Lee examines the eternal conundrum: a wicket-keeper who can bat, or a batsman who can keep?

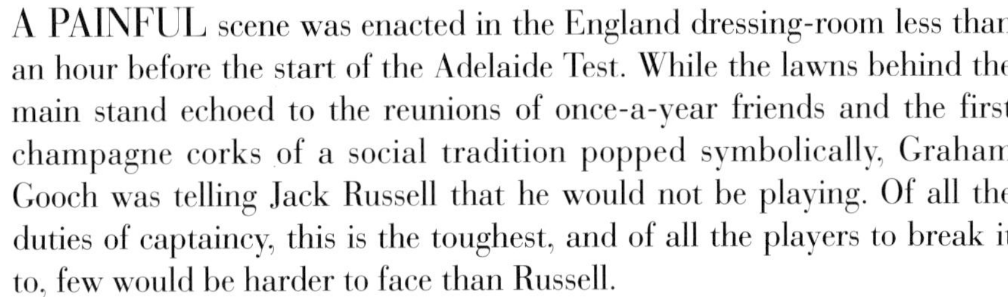

A PAINFUL scene was enacted in the England dressing-room less than an hour before the start of the Adelaide Test. While the lawns behind the main stand echoed to the reunions of once-a-year friends and the first champagne corks of a social tradition popped symbolically, Graham Gooch was telling Jack Russell that he would not be playing. Of all the duties of captaincy, this is the toughest, and of all the players to break it to, few would be harder to face than Russell.

It is not that he is a prima donna. He is nothing of the kind. Robert Charles Russell is simply the most obsessively dedicated cricketer of his generation, a man who by his own admission relegates everything else in his life to the status of a tailed-off also-ran. Cricket is his soul and his inspiration; keeping wicket for England his reason for being. Knowing all this, Gooch was surely weighed down by what he had to do.

Russell, of course, was not being omitted on grounds of ability, for both Gooch and Micky Stewart are forever labelling him the best wicket-keeper in the world. Rightly so, too. Nor was he left out on grounds of discipline – for histrionics on the field or for aerobatics off it. With Russell, the very notion is laughable. No, he was the fall guy in the ongoing saga of the missing all-rounder and the newly arisen dilemma of the half-fit seam bowler.

What it came down to was this. England was desperate to have Angus Fraser back in the side; his bowling is regarded very highly. But Fraser's chronic hip condition was a continuing worry and he could not be risked as one of only four bowlers. Because, broadly speaking, England's batsmen cannot bowl and its bowlers cannot bat, the only solution was to play six batsmen, five bowlers and no specialist wicket-keeper. It went against the grain for Gooch and, though he took it with stoic professionalism, it must have shattered Russell.

To this idiosyncratic little man, each Test match is a high point in his life and he prepares for it with such tunnel vision that, inevitably, he is thought eccentric. 'The lads call me "Top Drawer Loony",' he says. 'But I wouldn't say the things I do are eccentric. They are all common sense. I switch on to a Test match two days beforehand because it is so important. To me, it's a matter of life and death, you see.'

Russell had played twenty consecutive Tests since making his debut against Sri Lanka at Lord's in 1988. There had never been any question of dropping him; there still isn't. His omission was an indictment of what is missing in the English game and it is blackly ironic that, to all intents and purposes, he was left out to accommodate Fraser, in his way every bit as solid and professional.

There is a lot of the old sweat about Fraser. He rather resents being called old-fashioned but the label will stick, for his short hair, trudging walk and basic, accurate style of seam bowling make him a throwback to the days when Alec Bedser, so he will tell us, walked fifteen miles to The Oval and bowled thirty-five overs straight off. Fraser does have his histrionics – he is rather too fond of kicking the ground in self-disgust when he feels he has bowled a bad ball – but any who may have questioned his heart only needed to see him plough through twenty-six overs on the fourth day at Adelaide, the discomfort in his hip vying for prominence with a twisted right ankle, to be reassured.

Sorry pal: Jack Russell might well be the best wicket-keeper in the game but that wasn't enough to ensure his place in the team for the fourth Test.

Fraser, however, is typically English; no one would call him eccentric. It does not mean he cares any less than Russell, simply that he expresses it in a different way. Like Russell, indeed, he sets himself goals and broods when they defy him. Russell, although the consummate wicket-keeper, considers himself an all-rounder. His batting is important to him, just as it is important to England. 'I hate getting out,' he says. 'It hurts me badly. I feel agony inside. Some guys think you should just forget about it, but that is not my way. If I have lost concentration ... that's what really irritates me.'

Russell has kept wicket wonderfully well but he knew, and said as much, that he was one good innings away from having a really successful tour. Eventually, it was the absence of runs which cost him his place, the selectors regretfully deciding he did not warrant batting as high as number six.

So Jack sat it out, frustrated in himself but gallantly trying to uphold the spirits of others. As usual, he ate his staple diet of Wheatabix and bananas, drank gallons of water and thought of nothing but cricket. As usual, he repeated to himself that he aimed to play one hundred Tests, score five thousand Test runs and catch everything that came his way. Now, though, he knew that the state of his own team was going to make those ambitions just a shade harder to fulfil.

Crunch: The full power of Mark Waugh comes into play with this thumping square cut. The footwork might not be copy-book, but the roll of the wrists looks just fine.

Day one

Enter Waugh, Mark II

ALTHOUGH Mark Waugh had waited one hundred first-class matches and many thousands of runs for a chance at Test cricket, his debut century on the first day of the Adelaide Test was made with all the grace of a world-class batsman at the peak of his career.

Waugh's 116 not out off 144 balls was probably the most perfect piece of cricket played so far in the summer. What made it even better was that he came in at 4-104, all the top order (apart from the in-form Boon) having been dismissed by Malcolm, Small and DeFreitas.

When DeFreitas bowled Border for 22 and then was given a somewhat doubtful leg-before decision against Jones, who made a rare duck, England's gamble of playing five bowlers appeared to be working. But out strolled Mark Waugh who, to his third delivery in Test cricket, leaned gently on a fullish ball and blocked it down the ground for three. It was a delightfully easy shot and Waugh played in the same way for another three hours. His driving through the on-side brought to mind the young Greg Chappell and his cutting through the off-side was as convincing as that of his brother Steve, though more graceful.

Well played: Greg Matthews offers his hand to Mark Waugh, his New South Wales team-mate, after Waugh reached his century.

A measure of Waugh's dominance, despite the tense situation into which he walked so casually, was that Boon made 49 off 148 balls while Waugh made 116 off four fewer deliveries. Boon had been Australia's best batsman of the summer yet Waugh outscored him with ease.

Waugh's hundred was the fifteenth debut Test century by an Australian and the first since Wayne Phillips against Pakistan in Perth seven years earlier.

After Boon's struggle against the tight bowling ended with a lofted cut down to Fraser at third man, Matthews joined Waugh for an undefeated partnership of 145, of which a subdued Matthews contributed only 21. The usually extrovert all-rounder used his considerable energies to support and cajole Waugh on his way to three figures.

Waugh said Matthews, a New South Wales team-mate, had been telling him between overs to keep going, to keep concentrating. 'He said a lot of things. Some I listened to, some I didn't,' Waugh commented, in a gently chiding reference to Matthews's bountiful enthusiasm for the game and his colleagues.

As for his century on debut, Waugh said: 'Everyone is aiming to play Test cricket, and to score a century in your first game is something special. It was just one of those days when everything seemed to hit the middle of the bat.' As evidence of that, Waugh's second 50 took a mere 52 balls and he scored a spectacularly commanding 95 in the final session.

Like Greg Chappell and, presumably, other debut century-makers from Charles Bannerman in 1886-87 to Archie Jackson in 1928-29 and on to Doug Walters in 1965-66, Waugh looked like a Test cricketer as soon as he graced Adelaide Oval with his serene presence. No nerves were apparent despite the score-line. 'It's sometimes better to go in at 4-0 than 4-400,' Waugh explained. 'I bat a bit better when the pressure's on.' Waugh may *never* bat better and he said after play that he rated the innings the best of his twenty-six first-class centuries.

At the end of the Tufnell over in which Waugh square cut the boundary that took him to his hundred, his good friend and captain at Essex, Graham Gooch, went out of his way to shake his hand. Before the game Gooch had said that he would be happy if England bowled Australia out for 200 and Waugh made 100 of them. According to Waugh, as Gooch shook his hand he said: 'Well played boy.'

Mark Waugh, unlike Steve, who was thrust into Test cricket at the age of twenty, had been granted the time to grow into a man. That maturity and poise combined with beautiful footwork and formidable natural skill helped him produce one of the most memorable Test innings seen for some time.

For Gooch and England it was another reminder that while England's bowlers had done a decent job, having Australia in trouble at 4-104, Australia's depth had seen it through. The annoying thing for England was that Australia's top scorer had come from outside the team that had thrashed England in 1989. England did not appear to have that sort of talent *in* its team let alone outside it.

DAY ONE: Australia 5-269 (M Waugh 116 not out, Boon 49. DeFreitas 2-36)

FOR THE RECORD – DAY ONE

• Mark Waugh was the 349th Australian to play Test cricket.

• Mark Waugh was the fifteenth Australian to score a hundred on debut.

C Bannerman	165*	v.	England, Melbourne	1876–77
H Graham	107	v.	England, Lord's	1893
RA Duff	104	v.	England, Melbourne	1901–02
RJ Hartigan	116	v.	England, Adelaide	1907–08
HL Collins	104	v.	England, Sydney	1920–21
WH Ponsford	110	v.	England, Sydney	1924–25
A Jackson	164	v.	England, Adelaide	1928–29
JW Burke	101*	v.	England, Adelaide	1950–51
KD Walters	155	v.	England, Brisbane	1965–66
GS Chappell	108	v.	England, Perth	1970–71
GJ Cosier	109	v.	West Indies, Melbourne	1975–76
DM Wellham	103	v.	England, The Oval	1981
KC Wessels	162	v.	England, Brisbane	1982–83
WB Phillips	159	v.	Pakistan, Perth	1983–84
ME Waugh	138	v.	England, Adelaide	1990–91

Meet the press: What was it like, Mark, to go to the wicket at 4-104 in your first Test innings? 'I bat a bit better when the pressure's on,' said Waugh.

Day two

An evenly balanced match

LIKE A MARATHON runner slowly building up to peak form, England continued to improve on the second day in Adelaide with a steady performance against a hard-working but not dominant Australian team.

Two of England's best batsmen, Gooch and Smith, both due for big scores, were at the crease at stumps (on 50 and 36 respectively) with England 2-95 chasing Australia's 386. Gooch had looked in good nick for weeks and Smith was beginning to drive with more of his usual confidence. An evenly balanced match seemed the fairest assessment.

Although most people did not dare to predict a Mark Waugh debut double century, which would have been the fourth in history, there had been every chance he might go on to that remarkable achievement on the second day. When he resumed batting as serenely and comfortably as he had the day before, the odds began to shorten until Devon Malcolm ruined any such dreams with some hostile fast bowling.

After causing Waugh some trouble outside off-stump, Malcolm finally forced him on to the back foot to play a ball that lifted sharply off a length. Waugh could not adjust in time and he edged the ball down on to his leg stump.

Waugh's stand with Matthews had added 171 runs. On the previous day Matthews was the silent partner as Waugh cruised to his hundred, and he remained relatively quiet when Craig McDermott came out to join him. They added 60 in just under two hours and although it was not exactly exhilarating stuff it took Australia close to 400. Matthews made a valuable contribution with his 65 off 215 balls, again confirming the depth he has added to Australia's batting.

McDermott's undefeated 42 was a good effort; and in the evening session he took Australia's two wickets, Atherton having shouldered arms to an off-cutter and Lamb adjudged to have edged one through to Healy.

At that stage England was 2-11 and another collapse seemed imminent. But at last Gooch and Smith played well and the Australians did not look as penetrative as usual. Reid beat the bat several times and Hughes bowled with good pace and direction, but bowlers always have to prise wickets in Adelaide and, unless England reverted to its worst habits, it looked as though the Australians would have to work hard. Although Gooch had his worrying moments, in general he played comfortably, like a man who wanted to make the most of his chance to bat in Adelaide.

England had been looking a better side as the season had progressed and the feeling watching the team in Adelaide was that, having shaken off most of its injuries to key batsmen, it was finally coming to terms with the series and hitting something approaching the form and purpose that must have characterised its efforts in the Caribbean a year earlier.

Still, two injury worries clouded England's efforts on the second day. Spinner Tufnell did not appear at all because of a throat infection and Fraser, the side's best bowler, again stumbled on his ankle, aggravating the hip injury that kept him out of the Sydney Test. Fraser's diminished role was a big loss and significantly he bowled only seven balls to Mark Waugh in the innings.

Looking ahead, it seemed that by stumps the next evening, England would either be close to Australia's total or out on the field recovering from another collapse. From the evidence on the second day, the former looked more likely. And if so, a draw was already the favoured result.

DAY TWO: Australia 386 (M Waugh 138, Matthews 65, McDermott 42 not out). England 2-95 (Gooch 50 not out, Smith 36 not out).

IN PROFILE
Robin Smith

Born: 13.9.63

Tests: 23. Debut v. West Indies, Headingley,1988.

Highest score: 143 v. Australia, Old Trafford, 1989.

Nickname: Judgie because I have wavy hair and when it's long it looks like a judge's wig.

Favourite moment: When we beat the West Indies in Jamaica in the first Test in 1990.

Horror moment: Some time on this Ashes tour. Probably when I ran myself out in a one-day game in Brisbane. We needed 284 and I ran myself out for 6.

Greatest influence: Definitely my older brother Chris. He played at Hampshire with me and helped with technique and mental approach.

Superstitions: I did have a lot but I made a New Year's resolution to get rid of them. The only one I kept was the four-leaf clover I glue to the back of my bat. A lady at Hampshire once gave me one and I did well so I kept doing it. She grows them in her garden and when they wear off she gives me another one.

Favourite shot: The square cut. I get the biggest buzz out of hitting a square cut well.

How do you overcome nerves? I'm still working on that. I'm usually a jittery wreck when I walk out to bat. There's no real method to overcome them. I suppose it's just a matter of experience and telling yourself that in the end it's just a game.

Coaching tip: Perseverance will be rewarded. Play your shots with a straight bat and hit the ball hard but along the ground.

FOR THE RECORD – DAY TWO

- Mark Waugh and Greg Matthews shared a sixth wicket partnership of 171, the highest by Australia against England in Adelaide.
- Craig McDermott scored his highest Test score, 42 not out.

High and low: Craig McDermott and Geoff Marsh just couldn't be happier. Allan Lamb? He's not happy.

Disarray: Cricketers might wear well-creased, spotless gear on the field, but that doesn't mean the routine extends to home. In the middle of the mess is a happy Greg Matthews, after yet another superb fighting innings.

The changing fortunes of the Waugh twins

IF BARBARA Cartland had written the story of the cricket careers of the Waugh twins, Steve and Mark, even she would have been accused of stretching fiction beyond belief.

Word spread about these exceptionally gifted twins when they were still schoolboys. Although they represented their state at soccer and tennis as well as cricket, they chose the latter as their preferred sport. As they neared the end of their teenage years Steve, older by three minutes, appeared the tougher, more mature player. He made the New South Wales team before Mark and, soon after, the Australian team, despite limited first-class appearances.

As befits twins, there has always been a strange symmetry about the Waughs' careers. Steve's game matured first and, at international level, he blossomed as a superb one-day all-rounder – crafty, highly competitive and cool under pressure.

In manner, Steve has always appeared the tougher character. He has sharply focussed eyes and a mind that spots quickly any humbug or inconsistency. He never wastes words and speaks in clipped tones. Mark has always appeared more casual, freer in his everyday dealings with people, and less suspicious of those on the periphery of the game. This caused people to doubt his ability to handle the extreme pressures of Test cricket.

As batsmen, they are technically different. Steve favours the off-side and the back foot; elsewhere he can struggle to score. His movements tend to be exciting but abrupt and occasionally awkward. Mark is the opposite: stylish, graceful, with all the shots and the footwork to play them. Because Steve favours a few strokes almost exclusively, bowlers have worked him out. Mark's game is more adaptable and he has flourished accordingly.

Despite his shrewd, calculated appearance, it took Steve forty-three Test innings to score a century. It was a long wait and the sustained pressure of expectations finally took its toll on him this summer when he was dropped from the Test side.

At the same time, during the five uninterrupted years Steve was in the Australian team, Mark had been developing at his own more leisurely pace and his game gradually reached maturity after two highly successful seasons as a county professional with Essex.

Whereas Steve began the season under pressure to retain his place in the national side; Mark was out to prove wrong the critics who still doubted the depth of his desire to succeed. Mark was one of several contenders for a middle-order batting spot, should one become vacant; but

IN PROFILE
Mark Waugh

Born: 2.6.65

Tests: 2.Debut v. England, Adelaide, 1990-91.

Highest score: 138 v. England, Adelaide, 1990-91.

Nickname: Junior. I'm a few minutes younger than Steve.

Favourite moment: It would have to be making a hundred on Test debut.

Horror moment: Getting dropped from the New South Wales side after my first three games, in 1985-86.

Greatest influence: No one in particular. I had a few coaches along the way. Mum and dad helped a lot.

Superstitions: I always put my left pad on first and I don't like to change batting gloves during an innings.

Favourite shot/delivery: The best shot is the one that scores six runs. I suppose the square cut and the on-drive. My favourite delivery is the bouncer. Everyone says I bowl too short, so it has to be the bouncer.

How do you overcome nerves? There's not much you can do really. I don't read or anything. I usually feel like sleeping so I tend to start yawning a lot.

Coaching tip: Stay as natural as you can. Play your natural game.

just as it became obvious that the player most likely to forfeit his place was Steve, Mark moved well ahead of rivals like Tom Moody, Darren Lehmann and Jamie Siddons. When Mark faced the final challenge for a Test cap his class came through.

In mid-season, Steve and Mark's careers coalesced for 407 glorious minutes. Against a Western Australian attack that included Bruce Reid and Terry Alderman on their home wicket, the Waughs put on a record undefeated stand of 464 with a flawless display of unhurried, masterly batsmanship. Steve made 216 not out and Mark 229 not out. A month later, Mark was completing his debut Test century while Steve was playing club cricket for Bankstown in Sydney's western suburbs.

The Waugh twins' story has been a fascinating one so far and the remaining chapters will be no different.

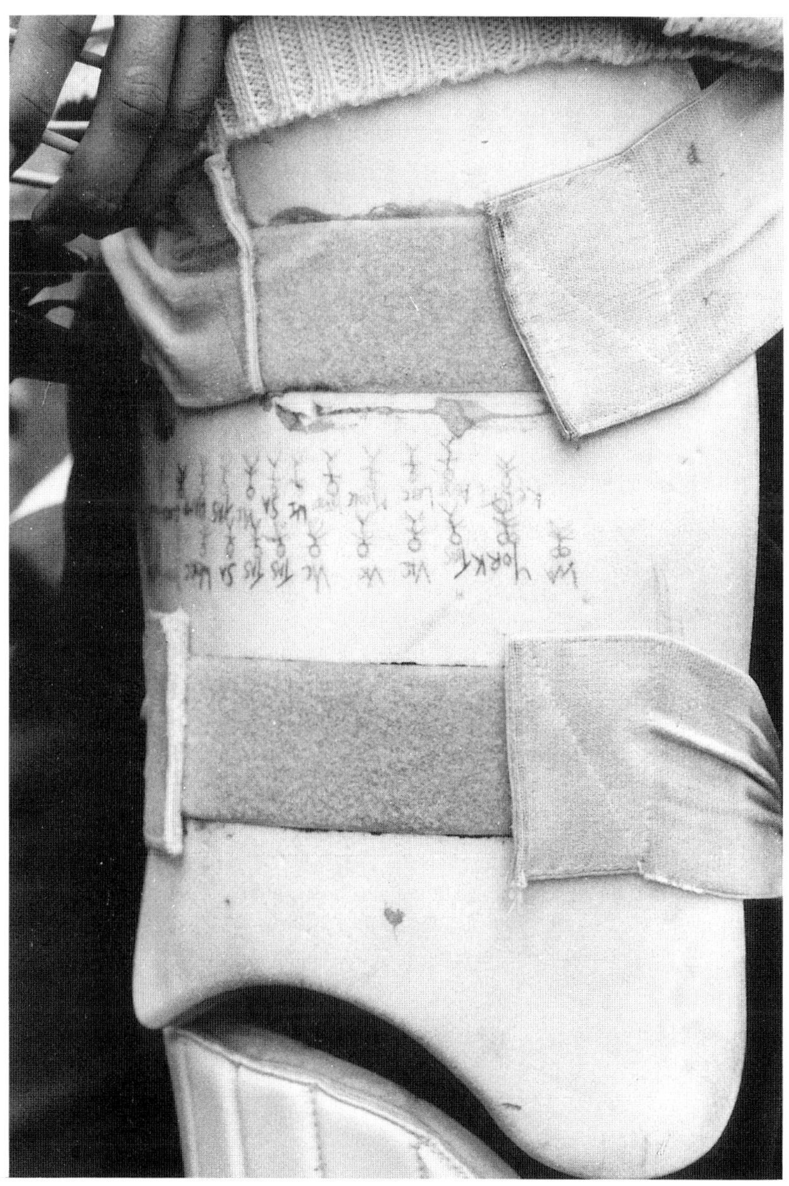

Notches: After each century, Mark Waugh notes the time and place on his thigh pad. He's running out of room. His debut test century was his twenty-sixth in first-class cricket.

Day three

England collapses

THAT OBSCENE eight-letter word, collapse, was on everyone's lips again on the third day of the Adelaide Test. This time England lost its last eight wickets for 92. From 2-137 England was all out for 229 and in serious danger of losing the game.

There are few sports in which mental weaknesses can be exposed as brutally as in cricket and a psychologist would have more than enough material from this Ashes series for a thesis on how international batsmen can lose their wickets so consistently, one after the other, when a modicum of pressure is applied.

Gooch and Smith batted on from the previous evening until Smith finally posted his first half-century of the series. On the next ball he was caught and bowled by Hughes and the wall began to crumble. Gower came in, the Australians set their leg-trap field and the enigmatic left-hander obliged off the last ball before lunch, clipping one off his toes straight to Hughes at deep backward square. Falling to an obvious trap off the last ball before a break gave the British tabloids another opportunity to stick the knife into Gower.

As well as some loose and spineless batting from England, the collapse was also due to some very good bowling from the Australians. In his first Test for two years Craig McDermott took five wickets, though it is fair to say he did not bowl any better than Reid or Hughes.

After lunch, Reid's angle from left-arm over the wicket caused some genuine havoc. In a devastating spell he dismissed Gooch (87), Stewart (11), Fraser (2) and Malcolm (2), each of whom was caught behind by Ian Healy when they failed to cover the angle or chased balls running across them towards the slips cordon. Those four wickets took Reid's series tally to 25 at the excellent average of 14.92. He was simply too good.

As England's batting again lived down to the lowest of expectations, its bowling undid some of that damage. At stumps Australia was 4-68 and the advantage won earlier in the day had been whittled away. Nevertheless the difference between the two batting sides remained: Australia had enough talent and spirit to recover from such a setback; England did not.

By the end of the day Taylor, Marsh, Jones and Waugh were all out – and in exactly the same manner as in the first innings. Taylor's dismissal gave him the quite bizarre record of having been run out in both innings of a Test twice, both times at the Adelaide Oval. When the fourth Adelaide run-out happened Taylor finally showed his frustration by angrily swinging his bat over the grass. Perhaps his luck would change when he got to the Caribbean.

PROFILE
Craig McDermott

Born: 14.4.65

Tests: 26. Debut v. West Indies, Melbourne, 1984-85.

Best bowling figures: 8-97 v. England, Perth, 1990-91.

Nickname: Billy, as in Billy the Kid, because I started fairly young.

Favourite moment: Winning the World Cup final in 1987.

Horror moment: Being dropped after taking 4-86 against England in Melbourne in 1986-87.

Greatest influence: Over the past two years, Jeff Thomson and my wife Sue.

Superstitions: I have a favourite World Cup shirt, the usual ACB shirt but with an extra World Cup badge on it, which I like to wear. If I get a lot of wickets in a first innings I'll wash the clothes I wore and wear them again in the second dig.

Favourite delivery: The unplayable fast out-swinging leg-cutter.

How do you overcome nerves? Just tell yourself to relax. Remember that you are good enough to be out there.

Coaching tip: Be as fit as possible and stay as natural as possible. Don't get caught up in too many theories.

V for victory: Craig McDermott's ecstasy can't be contained as another wicket falls.

Boon, who appeared to cause the run out, looked dejected at the other end. If he were in the England side he would probably have let it affect his concentration and cause his own dismissal. What was more likely from a player of Boon's experience and character was that he would make amends by scoring runs.

By the end of the day, Australia still enjoyed a lead of 235 with six second-innings wickets in hand. Unless the bottom half of the batting order caught England's collapse virus, some time the next afternoon Australia would have a formidable lead and then declare in order to expose England's disaster-prone batsmen yet again.

DAY THREE: England 229 (Gooch 87, Smith 53, DeFreitas 45). Australia 4-68 (Boon 24 not out).

FOR THE RECORD – DAY THREE

- Mark Taylor was run out in both innings. He was also run out in both innings against the West Indies in Adelaide, 1988-89.

My batting secrets: David Gower reveals all

From the square
David Gower answers the critics.

"ONE OF THE added dimensions of playing international cricket today is the obligatory presence of television cameras. While this is mutually beneficial to the sport, the players and the television companies, and absolutely essential to the many scribes who report on the game, one of the minor disadvantages is that, as a player, one is constantly aware of the rest of the world's analysis of one's technique.

Granted, it can be a benefit to a player, who is able to look at recordings of his performances and adapt things as necessary. Also, given that not everything that is said or written about players is inaccurate, there may be some commentary that can also be of service. The test of character is always when the five-hundredth person decides to pass on his criticism of that dreadful shot you played yesterday or last week and which was replayed round the nation twenty times in the next hour.

I think it is safe to say that, along with the compliments that have come my way, after the good days, I have had more than my fair share of armchair critics deploring my many methods of achieving my own dismissal. One week I am guilty of playing without due care and attention outside the off stump; the next a yet more heinous crime is committed outside the leg stump. I must admit that a lot of this is self inflicted, simply because I appear to do it all so casually.

What I can seldom convince people is that inside my head there is a lot more happening than is visible to the human eye and that I, for one, would be delighted to be able to achieve that extra consistency the cricket-watching masses crave.

But what is the key? We spend years training our instincts to be able to cope with everything that a bowler can send us at varying speeds from approximately twenty yards away. There are days when all that training seems to have worked, and others when you feel like a six-year-old looking for guidance on how to hold the bat. When things go wrong and you are forced to try to find a cause for your temporary (you hope!) lack of form, it is amazing how complicated the game appears, and how easy it seems to be to move your feet, hands or head at just the wrong time, instead of the whole process happening naturally and smoothly, which is the appearance when things go right.

There are a couple of other factors too, the crucial one being where and how the bowler delivers the ball. After all, he is trying to get you out, not just feed you runs! And do not forget luck. Just consider how unlucky a batsman feels to be caught by the only fielder for fifty metres, or how those watching gasp as the ball is hit hard but at catchable height through a ring of four fielders, safely allowing the batsman to continue on, perhaps to a century.

Because of all this, one has to learn as a player to cope with equanimity on good days and bad alike. Thus, while things were going well for me at Melbourne and Sydney, I was well aware that the next big mistake could bring as much flak as the two hundreds had generated praise.

I did not anticipate Adelaide to be the venue, but when an old bad habit reappeared and I managed to spoon the ball to deep square leg immediately before lunch, I had a feeling it was not a good move. Please believe me, this was not intentional; my instinct let me down – badly.

What puzzles me most though, is how on earth they let me play all those Text matches in the first place, if they knew I was going to do these things? ”

Me too, says David Gower: 'Inside my head there is a lot more happening than is visible to the human eye.'

IN PROFILE

Allan Border

Born: 27.8.55

Tests: 120.Debut v. England, Melbourne, 1978-79.

Highest score: 205 v. New Zealand, Adelaide, 1987-88.

Nickname: AB.

Favourite moment: There have been a lot of good moments, but winning the Ashes at Old Trafford in 1989 was special.

Horror moment: As far as desolation after a cricket match goes, the feeling after Headingley in 1981 when we'd lost a match we could have won and should never have lost, was the worst.

Greatest influence: In the early days, former England all-rounder Barry Knight at the Mosman club in Sydney. Later Greg Chappell. He got me to move to Queensland and Greg, his brother Ian, Dennis Lillee and Rod Marsh have all been confidantes. They were the sort of blokes you tried to have a beer and a chat with and learn as much as you could from.

Superstitions: None now. There was a period when I didn't shave during a game, but after a while I realised it was a bit silly.

Favourite shot: It's always nice to drive a bowler through the covers. Also the cut shot, though I seem to have lost that one a bit lately.

How do you overcome nerves? Through experience. On a physical level I've learned that it's hard to be tense if you deep breathe. Your mind might still be tense but you have to stop your muscles tensing up. I don't get as nervous now as I used to.

In the last years of your career, what shot would you most like to play? I'd like to hook Malcolm Marshall for six.

Coaching tip : When I've done some coaching the thing I've noticed is a lot of kids use a bat heavier than the one I use. Up to sixteen, you should use a light bat so you can control it. Then you just have to work at your batting in the nets.

Day four

Australia turns the screw

ENGLAND PAID for its poor first-innings total on the fourth day in Adelaide as Australia ground its way to 314 before Border declared, setting Gooch's side a quiet 472 to win in one hundred overs.

Despite being 3-25 and then 4-64, Australia was again able to recover because of its greater depth and determination. Boon continued his excellent form, scoring his ninth Test century with an assurance that belied the fact that he had struggled for consistent runs early in the season.

Boon is a very fine Test batsman – perhaps only now at the height of his powers. Before the summer, those close to him had suspected that his appetite for the contest had begun to wane. That suspicion had arisen after Australia's tour of New Zealand in March 1990, which had followed an exhausting programme: a ferocious series against the West Indies, the four-month Ashes tour of England in 1989 and the six Tests played in 1989-90, during which he had battled along with a bad knee injury. Boon had been tired and, like any family man, had been missing his wife and young daughter. A few months off – and a careful 94 not out in the second innings of the Melbourne Test – changed all that.

Compact in defence, powerful in attack, and able to play either way depending on the circumstances, Boon is a formidable top-order batsman. Perhaps his greatest strength is his temperament. Several bad stretches early in his international career hardened him and he now knows how to fight his way out of trouble. He is currently averaging more than 40 as either an opener or number three, which is a substantial achievement. That he has done it all from Tasmania, where club cricket and practice facilities are of a poorer standard than in the other capital cities, adds to that achievement.

On the true Adelaide wicket Boon's crisp, precise footwork allowed him to defend easily any reasonable delivery. Anything loose received the full treatment from his powerful, thick-set body.

Hughes, in as nightwatchman the evening before, also showed his value as a genuine Test player by making 30 and adding 66 with Boon before the latter was joined by his captain in a stand of 110.

There was a delightful moment during the day when David Gower chased a ball from the slips and, as he trotted back to his position, held his arms out like the wings of a plane and pretended to glide in to land back in his spot at third slip. Perhaps he had seen on the hill the English fan who had stuck a large inflatable jet liner to his sun-hat and was wearing a T-shirt that read: 'Gower's Flying Circus'. When the English lose their sense of humour they will really be in trouble ...

With Australia at 6-314 Border closed with less than forty minutes left in the day, a decision many people thought was unduly long in coming. At one stage, as he raced into the 80s with rare agression, it looked like Border might have been batting for personal reasons, chasing the Test century that had eluded him since 1988. But after he reached 83, having added 74 with Matthews (on 34 not out), Border waved to Gooch that it was his turn to bat.

Border operates on the theory that when you are well on top you should make the most of it, denying your opponents any hope of victory and so turning the screws on them mercilessly. He knows that it is easier for batsmen to chase a target that is within reach than merely to bat for survival for more than a day. As well, Border was worried about his bowlers. Hughes had a badly bruised backside after a collision with the concrete gutter around the boundary and Reid had the flu. By sending England in to bat late in the day Australia could have a quick burst at Gooch and Atherton without putting too much of a burden on its attack. Hughes and Reid could rest up overnight and arrive for the fifth day in better shape.

At stumps England was 0-19 and, although the wicket showed no signs of breaking up, form suggested England would be battling to last the full day and save this Test.

DAY FOUR: Australia 6-314 (dec.) (Boon 121, Border 83 not out). England 0-19.

Nice shot: David Boon had a marvellous series, and he was at his top in Adelaide, casually making the century after 90s in both Melbourne and Sydney.

Day five

Fast, furious, fizzer

THANKS TO another near-perfect Adelaide batting wicket and a brilliant opening stand of 203 by Gooch and Atherton, the fourth Test ended in the same way as the previous five played here, a draw.

After four consecutive half-centuries, Gooch made an imperious, attacking 117 off only 188 balls. At last he had made a Test century on Australian soil and given the country's cricket-watchers a glimpse of his power and ability to dominate good Test bowlers.

Atherton (87) gave Gooch admirable support and they added 96 in the first session in fine style. When Gooch was well caught in the gully by Marsh off Reid, Lamb blasted 53 off 54 balls and kept the scoring going at a hectic rate. England added 152 in the afternoon session but even so the target was still well out of reach. After a short burst with the second new ball Border called it quits at 5.43pm with England 5-335.

Border admitted later that he had been worried when Gooch and Atherton were in full cry and he was forced to spread the field to defensive positions. 'I've seen some terrible things happen in this game,' he said later.

Gooch revealed he had walked on to the field hoping only to bat out the day and save the match, but in the middle of the afternoon had begun to consider the remote possibility of a win. 'That's the way I play my cricket. I like to try to win games and I'm not scared of losing them.' Admirable words, but realistically England's first-innings failure had again allowed it only a gesture towards victory, never a genuine chance.

Australia now led 2-0 after four Tests and so had sealed the series.

DAY FIVE: England 5-335 (Gooch 117, Atherton 87, Lamb 53)
RESULT: Match drawn
MAN OF THE MATCH: GA Gooch (England)

PROFILE
Graham Gooch

Born: 23.7.53

Tests: 85. Debut v. Australia, Edgbaston, 1975.

Highest score: 333 v. India, Lord's, 1990.

Nickname: Zap after my Zapata moustache. Now it's just Goochie.

Favourite moment: Essex winning the Benson and Hedges final in 1979.

Horror moment: When our assistant manager, Ken Barrington, died during the Barbados Test match on our tour of the West Indies in 1981.

Greatest influence: My father, Alf; Bill Morris, my first coach at Essex; and later on, Keith Fletcher.

Superstitions: Nothing hard and fast. I don't like to change my gear too much when I'm scoring runs.

Favourite shot: The straight drive. There's no better sight for a batsman than to see the ball racing back past the bowler.

How do you overcome nerves? I've never really suffered from nerves. I always get a few butterflies, but you wouldn't be normal if you didn't feel a little apprehension.

What is the best and worst decision you've made as a captain? It's not easy to pinpoint those things. So many decisions go right and so many go wrong. A lot of it is educated guesswork.

Coaching tip: For players some way into their career, when you get set in an innings don't give it away. If you get to 30 keep going to 80 or 100. The next couple of times you bat you might get two good balls and miss out.

FOR THE RECORD – DAY FIVE

- David Gower (8048) passed Garfield Sobers (8032) to move into fifth place on the list of leading Test run scorers.
- Graham Gooch and Mike Atherton shared a first wicket partnership of 203, the highest by England against Australia in Adelaide.
- England totalled 5–335 in the fourth innings, the fifth highest total by England against Australia.

Run out of luck

From the square

Mark Taylor considers the game's fickle fortunes.

“IF EVER I needed reminding that I was having a rough trot this season, it came in the second innings of the fourth Test. Run out twice in the same game, and for the second time in a Test at Adelaide. That really hurts and it must be some sort of horrible record.

The run-out in the first innings was just a complete mix-up, nobody's fault. In the second, David Boon called me through, said 'no', then kept coming. I responded to the first call and by the time he said a final 'no' I knew I was gone. As I walked off I said to myself that I simply could not believe it. Unfortunately it was all too true and I was back in the dressing-room within minutes. In the first innings I returned to the viewing room very soon after my dismissal. This time I stayed on my own in the back room for a little while trying to come to terms with it all.

Getting run out is the worst way to get out, especially in Adelaide where you don't really have to bat all that well to get runs. As long as you can hang in there, the short boundaries and fast outfield mean you will get a few eventually. If you're hitting them well you can get a big score pretty comfortably.

I am a great believer in the idea that the wheel eventually turns your way. It has been one of those seasons when I haven't had as much cricket as I would have liked, a few decisions have gone against me that a year ago would not have done and I seem to be finding unlucky and odd ways of getting myself out.

But you have to expect that. I had two great years until this summer and I'm still hitting the ball well enough. In the nets the other day I remember thinking about what was wrong. I am using the same bat, the same pads and have the same body. So what is it? Probably nothing much with my batting. And after that second run out things cannot get any worse. I am due for runs soon.

I consciously try to stop myself thinking too much about what might be wrong. I remember seeing Graham Gooch getting Micky Stewart to throw him a hundred or so balls before the Oval Test in 1989. Graham had become very paranoid about playing straight and not getting out leg-before to Terry Alderman. With Micky he was concentrating on hitting everything dead straight. When he got out in the middle he hit his first scoring shot off the stumps through square leg for four. That is the way he plays and it is best to stick with it. Graham is a fine batsman and I'm not telling him how to play, but it is always dangerous to change too much.

I think everyone is meant to play a certain way and it is best to stick to that style. If you think too much about it you can get yourself confused and you end up forgetting what got you into the Test team in the first place, what got you all those runs. The simpler you keep your thoughts the better in the long term.”

A glimmer of light for England

ENGLAND PLAYED some good cricket in Adelaide, but again a poor first-innings total meant that any improved performances could only save England further embarrassment. One poor session against a good side like Australia and any chance of a win is forfeited.

Again England's poor fielding amazed all observers. Cricket manager Micky Stewart said after the game that his team included one or two players whose fielding careers up to this tour were 'a blank'. That was an extraordinary admission and confirmed Stewart's comment at the end of the fifth Test in Nottingham in 1989 that the gap between Test and English county cricket is far greater than the gap between Tests and Australia's Sheffield Shield competition.

But not all was doom and gloom for England. Gooch's 87 and 117 proved his class. Atherton and Lamb, the latter taking over the crucial role of number three, recovered well from first-innings ducks and Smith returned to something like his usual form with 53 in the first innings. Malcolm, Small and DeFreitas all bowled well at times but, without a fully fit Fraser, never seriously threatened Australia's batting.

Hmm: Devon Malcolm started the series slowly, gathered momentum, and finished as England's most respected bowler.

The worry for Border was that there were enough holes appearing in Australia's batting to suggest that the West Indies might be able to blast through in the forthcoming series. Border admitted that without Taylor and Marsh dominating at the top of the order, there had been more pressure on the much-vaunted middle-order. 'We've got off to dream starts over the past eighteen months. That hasn't happened this summer and the middle-order has been exposed. Jones has struggled as well. We are all going to have to knuckle down because the strength of the West Indies is that they bowl teams out.'

Border would have been aware that Devon Malcolm had caused the Australians problems with his pace and improved direction. He would also have realised that the West Indies would use not one genuine fast bowler but four. The Australians had been able to see Malcolm off, but against the West Indies the Australian batsmen would undergo a far more searching examination.

In the next match at the WACA, with its pace and bounce, Malcolm would be at his most lethal and Australia's batsmen further tested. How England's batsmen would cope with the wicket there was another matter. The odds were strongly in favour of at least one more collapse.

The view from home

The English view

Matthew Engel followed the Ashes series from the comfort of a warm bed.

"WHEN IT IS summer in Australia and winter in England, there is a time difference between England and the eastern states of Australia of eleven hours and a temperature difference that can be above forty degrees Celsius. This, more than anything, conditions the Pom reaction to an away Ashes series. The game goes on all through the long winter's night, from about midnight to seven in the morning.

Until satellite service came in on this tour, live television coverage was unknown. It was a radio story. But the BBC could usually only afford to give us the evening session. Traditionally we put the alarm on and listened drowsily, snuggling under the bedclothes while the frost built up on the window panes before the dawn and smug commentators talked of the heat and England's batting collapses. The first tour I remember was 1962-63, which happened to be England's coldest winter in memory. Australia sounded like heaven. Twenty years later, packing excitedly for my first visit, I was not even sure whether to pack a sweater.

In 1982-83, incidentally, the radio had started providing the first and last sessions. This meant that on one terrifying day in Adelaide, British listeners heard that David Gower was about 50 not out at lunch. The next news was that he was 20-odd not out at tea. The daft beggars had collapsed and followed on in the meantime.

There was no such problem this time, not with the radio anyway. The coverage was constant. Indeed, anyone who wanted to disfigure his house with a dish could sit up all night every night and watch television. It was not clear how it was possible to do that and do any work during the daytime or retain any shred of sanity after the battering to the senses from Channel Nine's commentators. And England's middle-order batting.

So I stuck to the old routine. Once I woke at about a quarter to three. After doing the things one does at that sort of time and then listening to the score I decided to check with the guys at the *Sunday Age* in Melbourne that they had received my weekly column all right.

'Ah,' came a voice from across the world when I got through, 'we've got three of your bastards out.' 'Four, actually. Gower's just out.' He thought this was hilarious and shouted across the room. 'Hey, it's Engel in London. He's telling us what's happening at the MCG. Gower's out.'

'Actually,' I said. 'I'm not in London. I'm at home half-way up a mountainside in Herefordshire. It's the middle of the night and there's a howling gale outside. And I'm still getting the news ahead of you.'

It was true that night but not on many others. Every time I woke up Gower seemed to get out. I began to feel responsible and started to sleep through. My wife was very grateful; I hope Gower was.

In my time, I have seen a lot of great sporting events but I shall remember the 1990-91 Ashes series very vividly. I wasn't there."

The Fourth Test
(Test no. 1162)

Australia v. England
Adelaide Oval
25, 26, 27, 28, 29 January 1991

Toss:
Australia

Twelfth men:
TM Alderman (Australia);
EE Hemmings (England)

Umpires:
LJ King; TA Prue

Result:
Match drawn

Man of the Match:
GA Gooch (England)

Attendance:
78,677

AUSTRALIA

FIRST INNINGS

Batsman	How Out	Ttl	Balls	Mins	4s	6s
GR Marsh	c Gooch b Small	37	67	93	5	-
MA Taylor	run out	5	18	19	-	-
DC Boon	c Fraser b Malcolm	49	148	191	4	-
AR Border (C)	b DeFreitas	12	33	75	1	-
DM Jones	lbw DeFreitas	0	3	2	-	-
ME Waugh	b Malcolm	138	188	237	18	-
GRJ Matthews	c Stewart b Gooch	65	215	318	3	-
IA Healy (+)	c Stewart b DeFreitas	1	6	7	-	-
CJ McDermott	not out	42	99	165	-	-
MG Hughes	lbw Small	1	23	30	-	-
BA Reid	c Lamb b DeFreitas	5	18	22	-	-
SUNDRIES	2b, 23lb, 2w, 4nb	31	818	584	31	-
TOTAL	**386**					
FALL	**11 62 104 104 124 295 298 358 373 386**					

BOWLING

Bowler	Overs	Mdn	Runs	Wkts	NB	W
Malcolm	38	7	104	2	2	1
Fraser	23	6	48	-	-	-
Small	34	10	92	2	-	-
DeFreitas	26.2	6	56	4	1	-
Tufnell	5	-	38	-	-	-
Gooch	9	2	23	1	1	1
OVERS	**135.2**					

SECOND INNINGS

Batsman	How Out	Ttl	Balls	Mins	4s	6s
MA Taylor	run out	4	12	22	1	-
GR Marsh	c Gooch b Small	0	5	9	-	-
DC Boon	b Tufnell	121	277	368	9	-
DM Jones	lbw DeFreitas	8	16	26	2	-
ME Waugh	b Malcolm	23	56	72	1	-
MG Hughes	c Gooch b Fraser	30	62	102	3	-
AR Border (C)	not out	83	148	224	6	-
GRJ Matthews	not out	34	51	71	1	-
SUNDRIES	1b, 7lb, 1w, 2nb	11	627	450	23	-
TOTAL	**6 wickets declared for**	**314**				
FALL	**1 8 25 64 130 240**					

BOWLING

Bowler	Overs	Mdn	Runs	Wkts	NB	W
Malcolm	21	-	87	1	1	1
Small	18	3	64	1	-	-
DeFreitas	23	6	61	1	-	-
Fraser	26	3	66	1	1	-
Tufnell	16	3	28	1	-	-
OVERS	**104**					

ENGLAND

FIRST INNINGS

Batsman	How Out	Ttl	Balls	Mins	4s	6s
GA Gooch (C)	c Healy b Reid	87	197	284	8	-
MA Atherton	lbw McDermott	0	16	21	-	-
AJ Lamb	c Healy b McDermott	0	4	3	-	-
RA Smith	c & b Hughes	53	149	200	4	-
DI Gower	c Hughes b McDermott	11	20	34	1	-
AJ Stewart (+)	c Healy b Reid	11	25	32	-	-
PAJ DeFreitas	c Matthews b McDermott	45	56	81	4	-
GC Small	b McDermott	1	16	23	-	-
ARC Fraser	c Healy b Reid	2	12	24	-	-
DE Malcolm	c Healy b Reid	2	8	10	-	-
PCR Tufnell	not out	0	3	12	-	-
SUNDRIES	1b, 3lb, 0w, 13nb	17	506	366	17	-
TOTAL	**229**					
FALL	**10 11 137 160 176 179 198 215 219 229**					

BOWLING

Bowler	Overs	Mdn	Runs	Wkts	NB	W
Reid	29	9	53	4	2	-
McDermott	26.3	3	97	5	8	-
Hughes	22	4	62	1	2	-
Waugh	4	1	13	-	1	-
OVERS	**81.3**					

SECOND INNINGS

Batsman	How Out	Ttl	Balls	Mins	4s	6s
GA Gooch (C)	c Marsh b Reid	117	188	214	12	-
MA Atherton	c Waugh b Reid	87	212	250	11	-
AJ Lamb	b McDermott	53	54	84	6	-
DI Gower	lbw Hughes	16	27	54	2	-
RA Smith	not out	10	37	81	-	-
AJ Stewart (+)	c Jones b McDermott	9	9	8	1	-
PAJ DeFreitas	not out	19	61	66	2	-
SUNDRIES	5b, 9lb, 1w, 9nb	24	588	381	34	-
TOTAL	**5 wickets for**	**335**				
FALL	**203 246 287 287 297**					

BOWLING

Bowler	Overs	Mdn	Runs	Wkts	NB	W
Reid	23	5	59	2	1	-
McDermott	27	5	106	2	8	-
Hughes	14	3	52	1	-	-
Matthews	31	7	100	-	-	-
Waugh	1	-	4	-	-	1
OVERS	**96**					

Wacko! Devon Malcolm bowled beautifully in Perth, and his head-to-head battle with David Boon was one of the highlights of the summer. In the end, Malcolm was the winner: Boon c Stewart, b Malcolm, 64.

Perth

THE FIFTH TEST

1 – 5 FEBRUARY 1991

DURING THE three-hour flight across the Nullarbor Plain from Adelaide to Perth, one of the world's most isolated cities, we were told that the temperature on arrival would be 44 degrees Celsius. The sixty-or-so English tourists on board gasped in awe and apprehension. In Adelaide they had complained that it had not been hot enough – not the sort of dry, hot Australian summer they craved. They were in for it now.

'We have not had enough fight and spirit to bring us through,' said Graham Gooch.

It would be tempting to say that the heat on the English cricketers was about to rise as well, but life for them could hardly have become more unpleasant. Admittedly they had drawn quite respectably in Adelaide, but on Perth's fast, bouncy wicket a draw was unlikely, and the chances of an England win as remote as the location for the game. The saddest commentary on the final stages of the series was that England's long-suffering supporters were more interested in the weather and the raging bushfires they could see from the plane than they were in the plight of their cricket team.

After struggling through the Adelaide Test, Graham Gooch's best bowler, Angus Fraser, was in doubt for the final match. A standby bowler, Phil Newport, had already arrived in Perth from Sri Lanka where he had been playing with the England A team. Or was that the B team? Newport had taken 11 wickets for Worcestershire against the Australians at the start of the 1989 tour, was picked for the first Test at Headingley on the strength of that performance and became one of several bowlers to suffer at the hands of Mark Taylor and Steve Waugh. He might bolster the number of fit men but he could hardly be expected to threaten any Australian batsmen. At least England still had Devon Malcolm, the man who had been fit for every Test and who had carried much of the bowling burden so courageously.

On your way, son: Merv Hughes worked tirelessly in Perth. This wicket of Mike Atherton was one of four in England's pitiful second innings.

Australia was likely to be without its spearhead, Bruce Reid, whose calloused heel was still annoying him. But the main reason he would be rested from his home Test was simply that he would be the crucial bowler in the Caribbean. Such was Australia's confidence that throughout the summer, especially in the one-day series, the selectors had used a rotation system among the fast bowlers in a bid to keep the top five or six relatively

Back: Terry Alderman missed the Adelaide Test with a minor injury, but wild horses couldn't keep him from his favourite WACA strip.

fresh for what would be eight months of demanding cricket. Without Reid, Australia could still beat England. But they would struggle to beat the West Indies without him, and it was thought prudent to rest him less than a week before the party left for that tour of tours.

In Adelaide Craig McDermott had taken five wickets in his first innings back in Test cricket and Merv Hughes finally had enough overs behind him to have found rhythm and developed stamina. Hughes had had a slow start to the season, perhaps as part of the selectors' ploy to keep him fresh for the Caribbean tour, where all his humour, aggression and general bluster would be sorely needed. He bowled very well in Adelaide and was reaching peak form at the perfect time for Perth's helpful pitch. Hughes had taken a hat-trick amongst thirteen West Indian wickets in Perth two years earlier and always bowled at his quickest and straightest on the WACA ground.

For Allan Border (keen to play despite a still tender tear in his groin) and his team the series was won, but there was still the motivation of winning their last game before the West Indies tour. For the Australians, form and morale were still important. For England, they were all but meaningless and there was an air of weary resignation about the England camp. The talk among the English press as they prepared their final, summing-up articles, was more of who would survive this tour than who would prosper from it. England had often been accused of lacking pride throughout the summer and now that pride was all they had to play for, any significant improvement was unlikely.

Day one

England's crazy collapse

AT LAST some variation on the familiar pattern. In Perth, England collapsed in the first innings, not the second, and on the first day, not the third or fourth. Otherwise it was business as usual.

Although the Perth wicket can be the best place in the world to bowl fast, statistics from recent Test matches suggest that unless there is plenty of moisture in the wicket on the first morning, it can be a lovely place to bat on the opening day of a Test. There had been no shortage of moisture early on the day before the match began, but by mid-afternoon the temperature had reached an all-time record for Perth of 45.8 degrees Celsius. If it had been in England there would not have been one refrigerator left working and, quite possibly, not one human being. At the WACA, there was little juice left in the wicket the following morning and on the evidence that in the past four Test matches there the lowest first-innings score had been 449, Gooch chose to bat when the coin landed his way. So far so good.

At 3-212 life for England was looking better than it had done since the second day of the first Test when Australia was bowled out for 152. Lamb and Smith came together with the score on 2-50 and added 141 in the best traditions of attacking South African batsmanship. Lamb was ferocious, taking to the bowling as if this was the last hurrah for England – which it was. Better to go down with a bang than a whimper. At the other end Smith was finally looking like the player who had dominated Australia's bowling in 1989. He moved from 46 to 50 with one of those technically perfect, savagely powerful square cuts that so typify his batting at its best.

When England arrived in Australia in late October, much was expected of Robin Smith. He had been the outstanding England batsman in the 1989 series. As well, he had played several years of club cricket in Perth and that, combined with his having learned the game on South Africa's fastish wickets, meant he should have been very well prepared for Australian conditions.

Smith made runs in the state games on this tour but lost all form in the Test matches. He is an open, honest man who readily confesses to suffering from chronic nerves which, in the past, have driven him to adopt a number of superstitions in an attempt to ensure success. This summer he became so burdened with worry that he tried to discard most of those strange practices – after all, none seemed to be working – but he kept the most unusual one, a four-leaf clover glued to the back of his bat. When it wears out, the supporter in Hampshire who first suggested the idea supplies another from her garden. Informed sources suggest she is developing a strain that will produce a five-leaf species to help Smith recover from this series.

With the ball coming on to the bat with speed and predictability and shots racing across a lightning-fast outfield, Border could do nothing to stem the flow of runs. For one of the few times in the series the Australians looked non-plussed. It was spectacular cricket but, for a change, it was all England.

By lunch it was 2-106, 62 of those runs coming in boundaries. Lamb and Smith added another 65 in the next hour and by tea it was 3-212, with Lamb on 91 and Gower on 12. Smith had gone before tea but Gower, starting only 66 short of Geoff Boycott's record for Test runs by an England player, looked intent on staying out there for quite a while. For more than three hours the Australians had been helpless onlookers and England looked set for a first innings total of 450 at least.

After tea, Lamb pulled at McDermott once too often and was caught at mid-on without adding to his score. As a forlorn Gower watched from the other end, England lost 7-32, its last six wickets for fifteen runs. Gower, playing recklessly near the end in a futile gesture towards that forsaken total of 450, was left stranded on 28 as England reached a pathetic 244 all out. For England, it was the fifth major collapse of the series and the most wasted opportunity of all. Unlike the Australians, no sensible rearguard batting from the lower order here.

IN PROFILE

Phil Tufnell

Born: 29.4.66

Tests: 4. Debut v. Australia, Melbourne, 1990-91.

Best bowling figures: 5-61 v. Australia, Sydney, 1990-91.

Nickname: The Cat, for a number of reasons. I'd like to think it was for my fielding, but I think it's really because I go out at night and sleep during the day.

Favourite moment: Getting five wickets in an innings in the Sydney Test. Another was walking out on to the MCG to bat when I had to hit a four off the last ball of the game to win. (England lost.)

Horror moment: None really. I don't look for any bad moments.

Greatest influence: MCC Young Cricketers, and John Emburey and everyone on the staff at Middlesex.

Superstitions: I always like to get a touch of the ball from the keeper as we walk out on to the field.

Favourite delivery: I always like seeing the arm-ball go. The best one on this tour was the ball that got Boonie in Sydney, caught at slip off one that spun.

How do you overcome nerves? I don't really think about nerves. It's a funny question really. If you don't, you don't. If you do, you do. I don't try to pinpoint any way of overcoming them. I go to sleep usually.

Coaching tip: Be accurate and consistent. Always give yourself a chance to wear down the batsmen.

Lesser teams might have given up the fight after tea, but the Australians stuck at it and were eventually rewarded. If there was one day which revealed the relative merits of the teams, this was it.

Wicket-keeper Ian Healy took four catches and continued to give his fast bowlers excellent support. Hughes applied tremendous pressure downwind, rising to the challenge like the accomplished Test cricketer he has become. He deserved a larger share of the spoils than two wickets and better scalps than Small and Tufnell.

McDermott confirmed his knack for taking bags of wickets by finishing with the extraordinary figures of 8-97. His final spell into the wind netted him 6-31 off 10.4 overs although his bowling was a mixture of short, wide deliveries and others of genuine pace and direction. A great result for McDermott, but even he would have admitted that as long as you got the ball down the other end you had a chance to take a wicket, such was England's unwillingness to dig in. 'I've got eight wickets but I've still got a hell of a lot of improving to do,' McDermott said after play. Still, the facts were there in black and white: in only three innings he now had fifteen wickets. And Bruce Reid was carrying the drinks!

For the England players it was a disaster and the deathly grey looks on their faces as they took the field said it all. At least they had the consolation of taking Marsh's wicket before the close, thanks to a fine delivery from Small. Australia ended the day 225 behind with nine wickets in hand and every prospect of another easy victory.

DAY ONE: England 244 (Lamb 91, Smith 58. McDermott 8-97). Australia 1-19.

IN PROFILE

Merv Hughes

Born: 23.11.61

Tests: 27. Debut v. India, Adelaide, 1985-86.

Best bowling figures: 8-87 v. West Indies, Perth, 1988-89.

Nickname: With the Australian team, Swerv. Also when I'm annoying him, Border calls me Gronk because he says I look like a caveman. When we're batting well and I'm bored in the rooms they call me Fruit-fly because I annoy everyone.

Favourite moment: The 1989 Ashes tour. Probably from that, the moment at Old Trafford when David Boon swept Nick Cook for the winning runs.

Horror moment: Getting dropped after my first Test. As well, some early back injuries.

Greatest influence: My father Ian and, when I first went to Footscray club, Lindsay James, Ken Eastwood and Ron Gaunt.

Superstitions: I like being the last out of the rooms when we're going out on to the field.

Favourite delivery: Anything that is fast and straight.

How do you overcome nerves? Everyone suffers from nerves because of the waiting around we do, but if you concentrate on the play, nerves fade. Nerves out in the middle are only self-doubt and the thing to remember is you got where you are because you were good enough.

Coaching tip: Get to bed early and have a go.

FOR THE RECORD – DAY ONE

- Allan Lamb and Robin Smith added 141, a record third-wicket partnership for England against Australia in Perth.
- Craig McDermott became the twelfth Australian to take eight wickets or more in an innings (8-97).

Well done, mate: Merv Hughes and Craig McDermott wrapped up England's second innings between them, Hughes (left) taking 4-37, and McDermott 3-60, which gave him match figures of 11-157.

Day two

England fights back

Model: David Boon is not trying to look cool: he's trying out the newest in on-the-field gear, wrap sun glasses aimed at reducing glare while fielding.

LED BY Devon Malcolm, England's bowlers salvaged something from the wreckage left by their batsmen when they bowled Australia out for 307 and limited the first-innings deficit to a modest 63 on an exciting second day in Perth.

Malcolm took three wickets but bowled better than those figures suggest on a wicket full of pace and intimidating bounce. It looked like Australia might have been forced to endure its third first-innings deficit of the series when Mark Waugh fell to Malcolm, making the score a perilous 6-168, but Greg Matthews, Ian Healy and Craig McDermott rescued the Australian side.

Matthews, batting with a torn thigh muscle, again held together the bottom half of the Australian batting with a measured innings of 60 not out. That took his series tally to 353 at 70.60; among the Australians, second only to David Boon. If a few of England's top order had put as high a price on their wickets as Matthews had in this series, England would not have been so embarrassed so often.

As happened in Sydney, Ian Healy played the adventurer to Matthews's straight man. In tense situations like these Healy always attacks and, against a fast, aggressive Malcolm, his innings of 42 off 57 balls was valuable beyond the numbers on the board. Healy added 62 with Matthews, and then McDermott, again displaying not inconsiderable skill with the bat, added another 51 with the all-rounder.

This series had been one that had followed a few set patterns: England's middle-order collapsing; Australia's top-order struggling, then David Boon and the lower order coming through. It was like that again in the first two days of this match. By the time Boon edged a full ball from Malcolm to keeper Alec Stewart for a fine 64, Australia was still only 4-113, Boon having contributed more than half the runs at that stage. Again Taylor, Jones and Border could not build innings and it was left to Boon to handle Malcolm with deceptive ease.

Boon is a fine player of fast bowling. Against Malcolm he was watchful and tight in defence to anything that warranted caution but he launched into any balls slightly off line or length with the knowledge that the fast

FOR THE RECORD – DAY TWO

- David Boon became the twenty-fifth Australian to score 500 runs in a series against England (530 runs at 75.71).
- Greg Matthews and Terry Alderman added 24, a record tenth-wicket partnership for Australia against England in Perth.

outfield would repay him in full. Boon's driving and cutting were at their best and it was a surprise when Malcolm induced an edge just when Boon looked set for another hundred. Still, while these two were at it, it was wonderfully exciting cricket; attack from both ends, with wickets occasionally falling around them. In many ways Boon and Malcolm were playing a separate game to the others and for a while it was quite riveting stuff.

Although Australia's lower order rallied well, the disquieting fact for Border was that, apart from Boon, the top six did not dominate as he would have liked. The West Indies has not *one* Devon Malcolm but four and without stouter resistance from the specialist batsmen the Australians would find life difficult indeed in the Caribbean.

The most telling dismissal of the day was the first. Taylor is renowned for having a temperament that allows him to play and miss at one ball, forget it and hit the next for four without a second thought. But this time, after sparring dangerously at Malcolm, he repeated the shot to the next delivery and was caught behind. When he felt the edge Taylor threw his head back in frustration. It was a rare loss of control for such a fine player and showed that the run of low scores he had endured in this series was finally affecting his even temperament.

For England, the second day in Perth was one of its more spirited efforts and after stumps Gooch would have emphasised to his team that it must bat in the second innings with the same conviction it had shown with the ball.

DAY TWO: Australia 307 (Boon 64, Matthews 60 not out, Healy 42. Malcolm 3-94.)

Day three

Another England disaster

JUST SO there was absolutely no chance that anyone would get the wrong impression about its batting, England conjured one more collapse on the third day of the Perth Test to all but hand Australia another gift-wrapped victory. During play a light plane circled the ground several times trailing a banner which read: 'Gower and Morris are innocent. OK.' As England crumbled yet again, perhaps a more appropriate comment would have been the title of the Sex Pistols' song about the Great Train Robber, Ronnie Biggs: 'No one is innocent'.

This time England was bowled out for 182, showing improved form by losing only seven wickets for 69 in mid-afternoon before Newport and Malcolm embarrassed their senior colleagues with a last-wicket stand of 38, the second highest of the innings.

IN PROFILE

Terry Alderman

Born: 12.6.56

Tests: 40. Debut v. England, Headingley, 1981.

Best bowling figures: 6-47 v. England, Brisbane, 1990-91.

Nickname: Clem, after the former Lord Mayor of Brisbane and Gabba curator, Alderman Clem Jones. Merv Hughes still occasionally calls me TMO, a name I got on the 1989 tour of England. It means Test Matches Only and I got it because I had the odd county game off in between Tests.

Favourite moment: It would have to be either the win at Headingley in 1989 or when we won the series at Old Trafford. I suppose the latter just makes it as the best.

Horror moment: That fateful day, 13 November 1982, when I injured my shoulder tackling an intruder at the WACA in Perth and ended up out of the game for two years. Actually the worst moment probably came a day or two later when I was told I might not bowl again.

Greatest influence: D.K. (Dennis Lillee). Watching him as a kid then training and playing with him for Western Australia, then for Australia. The progression was good for me.

Superstitions: Only one. When we're in a close-run chase I get very annoyed if people get up and move around the dressing-room. If they do, I shout at them to get back where they were and wait.

Favourite delivery: I suppose the Rob Smith/Mike Atherton one that swings late from leg to off and hits off-stump. Getting an edge through to the keeper is always satisfying.

How do you overcome nerves? Western Australia has had a psychologist, Sandy Grant, for a while now and he's been good. He has probably only reinforced what we do anyway – using key words, deep breathing – but it has worked.

Coaching tip: If you are getting a lot of coaching, make sure you find the points that best apply to you. I think there is a tendency these days to over-coach.

Australia was left 120 to win in two days play – but not before a rest day, and time to plan the celebrations. In the final over Taylor fell to a very good delivery from DeFreitas and Australia finished at 1-39. For Taylor, it was the end of a poor summer, one that was probably inevitable given his astonishing run-making efforts of the previous eighteen months.

The Australian pace attack was in its best form of the summer on this day and only three bowlers were needed to dismiss England. Alderman was back near his best form, confounding Gooch and Atherton with accuracy and late movement. Atherton tried his best to put his feet in the right positions but he was usually too late. Gooch's lack of footwork had not mattered much on Adelaide's friendly wicket, but in Perth his technical deficiencies quickly brought him undone.

The Australians passed several personal landmarks along the way. Alderman reached one hundred wickets against England in the equal-fastest time of seventeen Tests. The man he joined in the honours was the legendary Charles 'Terror' Turner, who made his debut in 1883. Hughes again bowled with fire and reached one hundred Test wickets in his twenty-seventh match. McDermott took another three wickets to post ten in a Test for the first time in his career. Ian Healy took another three catches to end the summer with twenty-four, an excellent effort; and Mark Taylor, at second slip, took two blinders to ensure England's end was not delayed unduly.

All over: Graham Gooch's great run ended in Perth. The quicker wicket exposed some previously hidden technical deficiencies.

Apart from Smith's 43 and Newport's 40 not out, England's batting was pathetically inadequate. Admittedly, the Australians were bowling and catching with tremendous vigour – presumably inspired by the prospect of returning home a day or two early before leaving a week later for the Caribbean – but England need not have obliged them so generously.

Some of the so-called senior batsmen gave the impression that if Hughes had sneaked up behind them and shouted 'boo' they would have bolted for the pavilion without daring to look back. Small seemed to use his time at the crease to express his feelings about his batsmen. He batted with the disgusted air of a bowler who has tried his best only to be continually let down by batsmen who lack anything like the skill and determination needed at this level.

DAY THREE: England 182 (Smith 43, Newport 40. Hughes 4-37). Australia 1-39.

Man of the Match: Craig McDermott's eleven-wicket haul was a career best. He had never before taken ten wickets in a test.

FOR THE RECORD – DAY THREE

• Merv Hughes, in his twenty-seventh Test, became the twenty-second Australian to take one hundred Test wickets.

• Terry Alderman became the tenth Australian to take one hundred Test wickets against England.

• Terry Alderman reached one hundred wickets against England in the equal fastest time of seventeenTests. The other bowler to do the same was Charles 'Terror' Turner, who made his debut in 1883.

• Craig McDermott, in his tenth test, took his fiftieth Test wicket against England.

• Phil Newport scored his highest Test score, 40 not out.

• Phil Tufnell scored his highest Test score, 8.

• England recorded its lowest Test innings in Perth, 182.

• Craig McDermott claimed the most wickets for Australia in a match against England in Perth when he took 11-172.

Breakdown in the batting engine-room

The English view

Alan Lee considers England's foreign legion.

ON THE very day that Mr F.W. De Klerk announced his intention to dismantle the apartheid system in South Africa, England began the final Test match in Perth with a side containing two South African batsmen and three West Indian fast bowlers.

England was breaking no rules with its selection and I am breaking no confidences by pointing out that it is not a unanimously approved policy. There are those who insist that the England cricket team is for those born in England only, and that there must be no exceptions. Less reactionary, but equally voluble, are those who distinguish between circumstance and forethought. In other words, no one who has grown up and been educated in England, and who regards himself as unchangingly English, can fairly be excluded from the England side for being born overseas. This group includes the three West Indian fast bowlers.

But what of the men who leave their homeland and go to England to play cricket? Men like Allan Lamb and Robin Smith, the two South African batsmen playing in Perth, and like Graeme Hick, the gifted Zimbabwian who was to become eligible for the England team in April 1991 and would undoubtedly play his first Test soon afterwards.

It can be said with confidence about all three that they would not have contemplated qualifying for England, by whatever means, if South Africa had been a part of, or even in sight of, the Test match circuit. Which is why Mr De Klerk's historic speech, and the Australian Prime Minister Mr

R.J. Hawke's swift and positive reaction to it, in which he proposed South Africa's reacceptance into cricket, created an appropriate moment to debate England's Springbok connection.

Those who believe Lamb and Smith, and their predecessors such as Chris Smith and Neal Radford, have no entitlement to an England cap must confine their quarrels to the registration rule book. The players cannot be condemned either for being born in a country outlawed from sport or for seeking another legitimate outlet for their talent. The law may be an ass, but that is not for them to judge. What is important is the contribution, both in terms of performance and unity, made by such players.

Neither Lamb nor Smith can be faulted here. Lamb is wholehearted in all that he does. Like many other South Africans he can be aggressive and unsubtle, and England's notion that he might have leadership credentials has now been fully exposed as nonsense. But he is a fighter on the field and a cheer-leader off it. Smith is in many ways a clone of Lamb, the difference being that Smith is more highly-strung and more analytical.

Lamb and Smith spent a lot of time together on this tour and had some melancholy matters to discuss. Indeed, having properly praised them for their efforts in recent years, and guardedly defended their right to be present, it must now be said that one of the powerful factors behind England's woeful failure in this series was the malfunctioning of the batting engine-room, the territory the South Africans have supervised in close liaison for some time now.

Lamb and Smith patently enjoy batting together, as was evident the first time they did so. Smith made his debut in the 1988 Leeds Test against the West Indies. He came to the wicket with England in a familiar mess at 80 for four and proceeded to add 103 with Lamb. When Lamb hobbled off with a torn calf muscle (of which, more later), Smith was out immediately.

Lamb and Smith only played once together against the Australians in 1989 but, again, both made runs. Then, with Lamb once more injured, Smith scored 553 runs in the series, a monumental effort in such a badly beaten side. Since then, Lamb has been troubled ever more by injuries, usually connected with his calf. When it failed him again, on his misguided jog back to the hotel in Ballarat before Christmas, it was a sign that England, and Smith in particular, would soon have to fend without him.

Smith, on the other hand, is part of the future, and to see his anxious struggle on this tour has been to suffer with him, so graphically does he live his batting both at practice and in the middle. His trouble has been confidence – his impulsive reaction to thrust bat at ball rather than play naturally. Only late in the series did he to any extent emerge from the trough. He made 58 and 43 with some of the powerful scything style of old. And, yes, he shared a first-innings stand of 141 with his chum Lamb.

Sooner rather than later, however, Smith may be the senior man in the engine-room, his new apprentice a chap named Hick, another for whom Mr De Klerk's reforms came too late to alter life's destiny.

Day four

Australia coasts home

Man of the Match: Craig McDermott walks off the field hat in hand, after taking 11-172 in Perth.

THE MAIN point of conjecture on the final morning of the series was whether the Australians would score the remaining 81 runs before lunch and so ensure a mercifully early finish. After all, some of us had planes to catch. Marsh and Boon did not disappoint. They needed only eighty-seven minutes against some ordinary bowling and the match was over half an hour before lunch on the fourth day.

With a handful of runs left, the Phil Tufnell fan club, a group of young England supporters who had laughingly wandered their way across Australia during the summer, burst into song. Holding their plastic beer cups aloft under perfectly cloudless skies, they sang in impressive chorus:

We're singin' in the rain.
We're singin' in the rain.
What a wonderful feeling,
We're hap-hap-happy again ...

The formalities that end a one-sided Test match often have a slow, strange, funereal air about them and this day was no exception. It all seemed a sad travesty of Ashes cricket history and something as Monty Pythonesque as the fan club's performance was probably the only 'sensible' response to such a poor England effort.

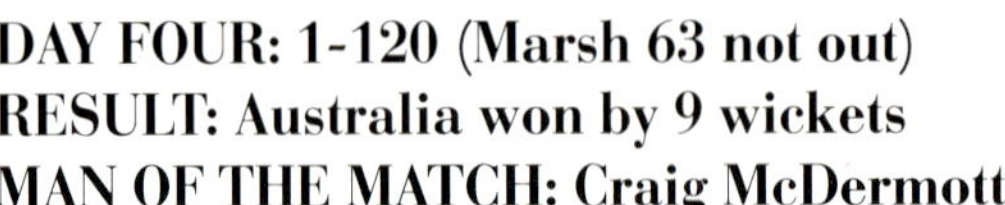

DAY FOUR: 1-120 (Marsh 63 not out)
RESULT: Australia won by 9 wickets
MAN OF THE MATCH: Craig McDermott

FOR THE RECORD – DAY FOUR

- Australia won the series 3-0. It was only the third time Australia has beaten England 3-0 in an Ashes series (1921, 1946-47, 1990-91).
- Allan Border had now captained Australia in thirteen consecutive Tests against England without defeat – a record achievement by an Australian captain.
- Ian Healy made his twenty-fourth dismissal in the series. This was the second highest number of dismissals by an Australian wicket-keeper in an Australia v. England series; Rod Marsh made twenty-eight (all caught) in 1982-83.

Sad, sorry: England's captain, Graham Gooch, spent much of his time in the field with a bemused look on his face.

Ian Healy comes of age

THERE IS a superficial fragility about Ian Healy's game that does not inspire confidence. He bats with an adventurousness that can seem like recklessness. His wicket-keeping can be loose around the edges although he rarely misses important catches. As proof of his growing maturity and comfort with his role, this summer he began to dive for wide catches that in the past he would not have attempted. In his quiet way, Healy developed a depth to his game that would be valuable to his side for several years to come.

Healy came into Test cricket in a similar way to Peter Taylor. Both were spotted and recommended by Greg Chappell when he was a selector: Taylor because of a dearth of good spinners and Healy because the temperament of his predecessor, Tim Zoehrer, was considered suspect.

With limited first-class experience, Healy struggled badly on his first tour – that arduous and controversial tour of Pakistan in 1988. In England in 1989 he suffered from lapses in concentration in county games, dropping too many easy catches; but, typically, he held everything that mattered in the Tests. Again, he did not inspire confidence, but the results were difficult to dispute.

Throughout his international career Healy has worked hard at his game. In Pakistan he disturbed team-mates' sleep by throwing balls against his bedroom wall to sharpen his reflexes. Eventually he was banished to hotel basements where he tuned up each morning with impressive dedication. That attitude has endeared him to his captain Allan Border and coach Bob Simpson.

This summer Healy had been more settled, seeing himself as an accepted member of a successful team. His catching was excellent and, although he would struggle to produce as brilliant an individual highlight as Jack Russell's stumping of Dean Jones in the Sydney Test, he provided impressively reliable support for his fast bowlers. His twenty-four catches prove that.

Healy's batting was also a source of strength to the Australians. He has never lacked for courage, as was shown when he took two savage blows to that most vulnerable of regions in consecutive deliveries from Curtley Ambrose in the Melbourne Test of 1988-89. This summer Healy averaged 25, with a highest score of 69, made when he helped Australia avoid possible defeat in the tense second innings in Sydney. Healy's batting is always aggressive and, although there are times when his spirit of adventure makes the heart beat too quickly, he always plays with courage and the competitive edge that so distinguished the Australians from their opponents in this series.

The one aspect of Healy's game that could be toned down is his appealing. Although it is part of a wicket-keeper's job to support his bowlers' appeals, Healy tends to overdo it and to over-react when those appeals are turned down. In this he is reflecting modern fashion, but that is no excuse.

Loser, winner: Jack Russell (left) will look back on the series with horror. But for his counterpart, Ian Healy, it was a triumph.

Gooch talks tough

AFTER THE match, members of both teams swapped shirts, jumpers and caps in the dressing-rooms, while upstairs in the public world of the media, Graham Gooch and Micky Stewart were put through the most intense gruelling of the summer. The press conference lasted some forty-five minutes and Gooch agreed the tour had been 'a nightmare'. 'I'm gutted, really disappointed,' he said. 'At the end of the day I feel responsible. I failed to get the best out of my players and have been unable to motivate them sufficiently. We have to find people who really want to play for England, people who are willing to give their best at all times. We have not come through in tight situations and we have not had, in my opinion, enough fight and spirit to bring us through. It's those players (on this tour) whose careers will suffer. They won't make it – and they've only got themselves to blame.'

Stewart and Gooch noted that Australians, at all levels, play 'life or death' cricket. England's gentleman cricketers of old had often complained of Australian over-competitiveness; but now that the game is professional, especially in England, one would expect players to try hard, to be able to cope with pressure. Gooch and Stewart admitted that their team had not been able to do that.

Although he was accused of distracting attention from his own role in the whole sorry saga, Stewart made sense when he said many of his players had been amazed at the higher standards of the game in Australia, even at district level. He had long advocated a change to four-day county cricket and did so again after the match. Anyone who has watched two middle-of-the-road county teams going lazily through the motions on yet another day at the office at some empty county ground would have to agree about the need for change in English cricket.

Allan Border said his side had performed better in Perth than at any time in the series, no doubt as a result of his comment after the Adelaide Test that Australia would have to improve if it were to challenge the West Indies. Without being dismissive, he said the England team had provided the Australians with a good warm-up for the West Indies tour. 'Their bowling has not let them down,' he said. 'They kept us under pressure.' So they had, but England's batting could not remotely match its bowling and in the end Australia had cruised to an easy series win.

IN PROFILE

Ian Healy

Born: 30.4.64

Tests: 26. Debut v. Pakistan, Karachi, 1988.

Best figures: 69 v. England, Sydney, 1990-91. 5 catches in an innings v. England, Melbourne, 1990-91.

Nickname: Heals and Savlon, which usually comes before Heals.

Favourite moment: Winning the first Test in the 1989 Ashes series at Headingley.

Horror moment: Feeling pretty awful after being hit three times in a tender spot by Curtley Ambrose in the Melbourne Test in 1988-89.

Greatest influence: My older brother Greg. He represented Queensland in junior cricket and played first grade in Brisbane, but gave it away when he was about twenty-five.

Superstitions: None. But I realise the game has got to have them.

Favourite wicket-keeping effort: A catch like the left-handed diving one I took in Melbourne in 1989-90 to dismiss Wasim Akram.

How do you overcome nerves? You only get nervous if you're not concentrating. Once you are out in the middle concentrating on the game, nerves fade.

Coaching tip: Know the basics and work hard on them. And make sure you enjoy yourself.

Happy days: Geoff Marsh had a bitsy series, but he had plenty to laugh about in Perth – an Australian 3-0 series win, and 63 not out.

Facing new tactics

From the square

Mark Taylor ruminates on how England bowled around the wicket to him.

"THE PERTH WICKET is always a great place for a fast bowler and a demanding pitch for an opening batsman. With Devon Malcolm bowling with speed in this match, it was also the best place for all the Australians to play their last game before going to the West Indies, where the wickets would not be as fast or bouncy, but where there would be four fast bowlers not just one.

Overall Devon was England's best bowler this summer. He is quite fast and has excellent stamina; and although he is probably not as consistent and testing as Angus Fraser, in this series he played all the matches while Angus missed two. Facing him was a good preparation for what we would cop in the Caribbean.

For me the Perth Test was typical of my whole series. Once again I managed to reach double figures only to play a bad shot in the first innings and receive a good ball in the second. An aggregate of 200-odd for five Tests is by no means a great tally, but I suppose I was due for a few low scores. At least I was part of a winning team, which always provides the most satisfaction.

England's tactic of bowling around the wicket to me this summer worked pretty well. I made two 60s early on but even then was out cutting twice in the first four innings. When they got me out, caught in the gully, in the first innings in Brisbane they must have thought they were on to something. Even though I hit Devon Malcolm for a couple of fours through there in the second innings and thought I was starting to counter the tactic quite well, I expected them to persist with it.

England had to try something different against me. After scoring runs on the tour in 1989, I knew they would try to work out a tactic to upset me. But I don't think they are really trying to get me out cutting. What they are doing is trying to restrict my scoring and so frustrate me out. In the 1989 series, they bowled all over the place to me, but in this series they are obviously concentrating on keeping the ball wide outside my off-stump and fairly full of length so I will be forced to chase the ball.

I didn't do too much work to counter the tactic. Occasionally in the nets I asked the bowlers to come around to me, and when a few asked if the tactic was worrying me I just said it seemed pointless them bowling over the wicket when it looked like I wasn't going to face that sort of bowling in the Tests.

In the middle I just tried to be more selective. I concentrated on choosing the right balls to attack and playing straight and hoped that if I did get a few away to the fence they would change their angle. The main thing was not to think too much about it.

I consciously try to stop myself thinking too much about what might be wrong with my batting. I think everyone is meant to play a certain way

Rare sight: Mark Taylor dominated England's bowlers in 1989; not so in 1990-91. The around-the-wicket tactic adopted by Angus Fraser and Devon Malcolm had something to do with it, but there was also that missing element of luck – every batsman needs it.

and it is best to stick to that style. If you think too much about it you can get yourself confused and you end up forgetting what got you into the Test team in the first place – what got you all those runs. The simpler you keep your thoughts, the better in the long term.

I'd also have to say that I don't think England bowled as well to some of our other players. They tended to bowl towards David Boon's legs and that cost them a lot of runs. This often happens. When bowlers concentrate on one or two batsmen they tend to forget the others. With a strong batting line-up like ours, those other batsmen can compensate for any difficulties their colleagues might be having.

To sum up the series, I think it was fairly even on a player-by-player basis. The reason we won so comfortably was that when crunch periods came in each match we were by far the better side.

We have now beaten England well in the past two series and we beat Pakistan 1-0 in a three-Test series last summer. We know how to win now and it would be up to us to lift an extra percentage to cope with the West Indies away from home. It would be very difficult but there is a great spirit in this Australian team and, all things considered, we could not have hoped for a better preparation. ”

The art of the cricket tour

The English view

How David Gower found himself in the cockpit of a Tiger Moth.

“ PEOPLE often ask, when you have finally persuaded them to get off the subject of your batting, how you are enjoying the tour. The official answer in 1990-91 has generally been along the lines of 'Fine, thank you, but it would be nicer to be winning'. That was the reason we all came to Australia, to try to win the Test series and thus regain the Ashes, and there is no doubt that winning helps make all the little problems disappear.

Australia remains the tour that English professionals most like to take part in. Everyone is aware of the Australian tradition of a high standard of play on the field and plenty to do off it, if you can find the time.

The fact is that, with the job paramount in everyone's mind, little things like nets and training take precedence over sight-seeing and, on a tour, the likelihood is that there is plenty of work being done in between matches to try to produce the desired results.

Travel is said to broaden the mind. Touring tests the patience. Moving twenty people or more, plus over a hundred pieces of baggage is never easy. Our itinerary on this tour has meant that on several occasions the team left for the next venue the same night as the previous game had finished. When a refuellers' strike diverted our plane to Alice Springs en route to Perth, we did not exactly arrive on time, and took the next day to unwind both from the Test match we had just finished and the journey.

This can all add up to a certain degree of stress – part of the job certainly – but, one is told, the way things have to be today. In truth, one is glad that air travel is largely so efficient, even if the pace of touring in the old days seems to have been a little more relaxed – as it does especially when the World Series is in progress and it is only worth unpacking the very top layer of the suitcase at each stop.

Of course, at some stage or other, something has to be said or done to relieve the pressure. Cricket sides have always survived on a sense of humour, allied to a certain sense of opportunism, and the odd prank never goes entirely amiss, whether it be Ian Botham's old favourite of setting fire to the newspaper you were reading or something more substantial.

Hence, when the situation arose at the Gold Coast that we were playing at a ground literally two minutes from an airfield from which two Tiger Moths could be chartered for sightseeing at very reasonable rates, here was an opportunity apparently too good to miss. Robin Smith and Allan Lamb had been given orders to bat until tea, so I could not resist the temptation to ask the pilots to take us over the stadium – and the lower the better. My flight lieutenant was John Morris and it is now history that we buzzed the ground at a time, we could say later, that we were celebrating Robin Smith's first century for England abroad.

Understandably, management took a dim view and imposed the maximum penalty which made it a very expensive flight, but the opportunity had been there and many people did enjoy it.

Another opportunity of a less controversial nature arrived earlier in the tour, with time off being granted by a more understanding management when I needed to rest a wrist injury after the last World Series match. My girlfriend, Thorunn, and I took this opportunity to accept an invitation to visit the centre of Australia, Alice Springs and Ayers Rock. Again, it was a chance too good to miss and, for any doubters, let me say it is well worth the effort to climb the rock and appreciate its awesome size.

In essence, you have to make the most of the chance to tour, wherever the destination. Certainly, the job has to come first, and success or failure will have a big effect on everything else that happens. Whatever problems there are always fade into the background, especially when the day comes to fly home and you realise that it was not too bad after all and promise to give yourself the chance to come back again. ”

Those magnificent men: David Gower's view of the famous flight over Carrara was this: 'The odd prank never goes entirely amiss.'

The Fifth Test

Test No. 1164

Australia v. England
WACA Oval, Perth
1, 2, 3, 5 February 1991

Toss:
England

Twelfth Men:
BA Reid (Australia);
MP Bicknell (England)

Umpires:
SG Randell;
CO Timmins

Result:
Australia won by 9 wickets

Man of the Match:
CJ McDermott (Australia)

Attendance:
44,539

ENGLAND

FIRST INNINGS

Batsman	**How Out**	**Ttl**	**Balls**	**Mins**	**4s**	**6s**
GA Gooch (C)	c Healy b McDermott	13	33	39	2	-
MA Atherton	c Healy b McDermott	27	44	62	4	-
AJ Lamb	c Border b McDermott	91	122	206	13	1
RA Smith	c Taylor b McDermott	58	121	153	9	1
DI Gower	not out	28	52	94	3	-
AJ Stewart (+)	lbw McDermott	2	9	9	-	-
PAJ DeFreitas	c Marsh b McDermott	5	8	7	-	-
PJ Newport	c Healy b McDermott	0	1	1	-	-
GC Small	c Boon b Hughes	0	4	5	-	-
PCR Tufnell	c Healy b Hughes	0	3	5	-	-
DE Malcolm	c Marsh b McDermott	7	12	27	1	-
SUNDRIES	1b, 6lb, 1w, 5nb	13	409	313	32	2
TOTAL		**244**				
FALL	**27 50 191 212 220 226 226 227 277 244**					

BOWLING

Bowler	**Overs**	**Mdn**	**Runs**	**Wkts**	**NB**	**W**
Alderman	22	5	66	-	-	-
McDermott	24.4	2	97	8	5	-
Hughes	17	3	49	2	-	1
Waugh	1	-	9	-	-	-
Matthews	2	-	16	-	-	-
OVERS	**66.4**					

SECOND INNINGS

Batsman	**How Out**	**Ttl**	**Balls**	**Mins**	**4s**	**6s**
GA Gooch (C)	c Alderman b Hughes	18	62	91	2	-
MA Atherton	c Boon b Hughes	25	109	158	2	-
AJ Lamb	lbw McDermott	5	11	16	1	-
RA Smith	lbw Alderman	43	70	108	7	-
DI Gower	c Taylor b Alderman	5	6	7	1	-
AJ Stewart (+)	c Healy b McDermott	7	18	42	1	-
PAJ DeFreitas	c Healy b Alderman	5	9	14	-	-
PJ Newport	not out	40	55	63	6	-
GC Small	c Taylor b Hughes	4	12	20	1	-
PCR Tufnell	c Healy b Hughes	8	11	10	1	-
DE Malcolm	c Jones b McDermott	6	12	31	-	-
SUNDRIES	5b, 5lb, 0w, 6nb	16	375	294	22	-
TOTAL		**182**				
FALL	**41 49 75 80 114 118 125 134 144 182**					

BOWLING

Bowler	**Overs**	**Mdn**	**Runs**	**Wkts**	**NB**	**W**
McDermott	19.3	2	60	3	4	-
Alderman	22	3	75	3	2	-
Hughes	20	7	37	4	-	-
OVERS	**61.3**					

AUSTRALIA

FIRST INNINGS

Batsman	How Out	Ttl	Balls	Mins	4s	6s
GR Marsh	c Stewart b Small	1	10	10	-	-
MA Taylor	c Stewart b Malcolm	12	45	83	-	-
DC Boon	c Stewart b Malcolm	64	124	148	10	-
AR Border (C)	lbw DeFreitas	17	22	48	3	-
DM Jones	b Newport	34	52	73	5	-
ME Waugh	c Small b Malcolm	26	37	60	4	-
GRJ Matthews	not out	60	137	196	5	-
IA Healy (+)	c Lamb b Small	42	57	74	5	-
CJ McDermott	b Tufnell	25	46	73	3	-
MG Hughes	c Gooch b Tufnell	0	4	6	-	-
TM Alderman	lbw DeFreitas	7	21	25	1	-
SUNDRIES	2b, 8 lb, 1w, 8nb	19	555	406	36	-
TOTAL	**307**					
FALL	**1 44 90 113 161 168 230 281 283 307**					

BOWLING

Bowler	Overs	Mdn	Runs	Wkts	NB	W
Malcolm	30	4	94	3	-	-
Small	23	3	65	2	-	1
DeFreitas	16.5	2	57	2	2	-
Newport	14	-	56	1	6	-
Tufnell	7	1	25	2	-	-
OVERS	**90.5**					

SECOND INNINGS

Batsman	How Out	Ttl	Balls	Mins	4s	6s
MA Taylor	c Stewart b DeFreitas	19	36	54	3	-
GR Marsh	not out	63	110	141	10	-
DC Boon	not out	30	45	87	3	-
SUNDRIES	0b, 5lb, 2w, 1nb	8	191	141	16	-
TOTAL	**1 wicket for**	**120**				
FALL	**39**					

BOWLING

Bowler	Overs	Mdn	Runs	Wkts	NB	W
Malcolm	9	-	40	-	-	-
Small	10	5	24	-	-	2
DeFreitas	6.2	-	29	1	1	-
Newport	6	-	22	-	-	-
OVERS	**31.2**					

THE LAST WORD

Border's competitive, no-nonsense team reflects his own style of play. He and Australia now faced the fiercest campaign of all, the West Indies in the Caribbean.

THREE HOURS after the end of the fifth Test match, the Australians were on their way home. They had five days of relaxation before gathering in Sydney for a black-tie dinner then flying to the West Indies via London the following morning. As Allan Border had noted at the end of the Perth Test, the Ashes series had provided the Australians with a good (though hardly demanding) preparation for the Caribbean campaign.

England's loss in four days in Perth gave the Englishmen a free day at the beach before leaving for three one-day internationals over two weeks in New Zealand. If ever a cricket team wanted to return to the emotional and physical comforts of home, it must surely have been this England side. But, as is usually the case these days, they had one more short tour added to what had already been a hectic four months. Not surprisingly, England managed to lose the New Zealand series as well, collapsing one last time in the final, deciding game.

Just as the disparate quality of play reflected the large gap between the Australian and England teams, so the series result reflected the vastly different fortunes of Australian and English cricket at the start of the 1990s. After the encouraging performance of Graham Gooch's revamped team in the West Indies in early 1990, the Englishmen were going home beaten comprehensively in another Test series. As Australia waged the fiercest cricket campaign of all, playing the West Indies in the West Indies, England faced another few months of soul-searching before preparing to face Viv Richards' team again. Another hiding and there would be no place to turn to for Gooch, Ted Dexter and Micky Stewart.

Border, after five years of painful rebuilding, was finally going to the Caribbean with a decent chance of victory. He has gathered around him the sort of competitive, no-nonsense team that reflects his own style of play. Border has already said he wants to return to England in 1993 for one more Ashes series, but that must surely be the end of his Test career – one of the longest and most productive in the history of the game.

For Gooch, as competitive and committed as his friend Border, his term as captain had seen little achieved. After a promising start to the decade, there could be no doubting that England faced troubled times as it looked deep within its tortured soul for the reasons behind a dispirited and debilitating performance.

Reflections: Allan Border and Graham Gooch might be rivals on the field, but they are the best of mates when it's all over. The pair played together for several seasons at Essex.

Final reflection

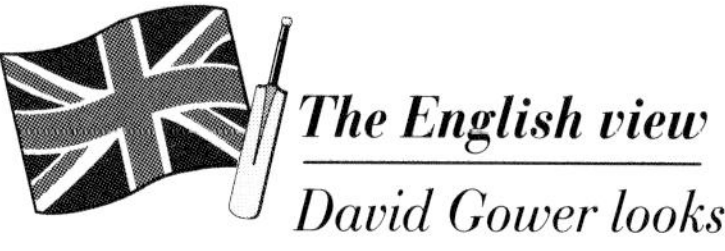

The English view

David Gower looks back on the tour and asks how can England develop 'that winning feeling'?

"IT IS NOT a huge amount of fun having to reflect on a tour that basically did not go according to plan. Inevitably in October people were talking about two evenly matched teams and hesitating to predict the outcome of the series with any confidence. Both captains were bullish yet modest in their own predictions though, of course, both would have had high hopes of glory.

Three and a half months later it was we, the visitors, who had to rue the lost opportunities, while our hosts took what little time was available before their next mission in the West Indies to savour a job well done and a series victory by a more than comfortable margin.

Smile please: David Gower and Greg Matthews exchange one-liners for the camera after the last Test. It was Matthews who removed Gower in the Melbourne Test, for his first duck in 119 Test innings.

It seems that the single factor that divided the teams was the Australians' ability to cope with the pressure situations. Simply, whenever a game reached a crisis point, it was the English who folded and the Australians who prospered, or even the Kiwis who climbed over us into the one-day finals. Hence, at the end of the series, Graham Gooch was left to question his team's attitude and competitive spirit.

He obviously had a point, but the problem is how to rectify this apparent deficiency, given that the methods and approach of both sides are not dissimilar. Both captains and managers are keen on hard work and discipline as a basic modus operandi. So why did an England side that looked so impressive in the field on the second day of the series in Brisbane when it bowled Australia out so cheaply, finish up being described by its own captain as one of the worst fielding sides in history?

Admittedly, the actual result of winning matches is a great boon to a team's confidence. Despite the losses in Brisbane and Melbourne, we have to rue one or two missed chances in Sydney that could conceivably have brought victory and kept our series hopes alive. Even in Adelaide, with Australia five wickets down and with another sniff of a chance to develop a winning position, it was Mark Waugh who soaked up the pressure and denied us that opening.

In many ways the Perth Test summed up the series. The final session of the first day saw England collapse in a hurry after Lamb and Smith, the men who until then had suffered either fitness or form problems, had batted brilliantly through the afternoon. When Australia batted and lost wickets, again the lower order added valuable runs to take them to a comfortable lead; with Matthews, outstanding in his application, ably assisted by McDermott. Those extra runs could have been vital in a closer contest but, as it turned out, the rest of the game belonged entirely to Australia in any case. Any references to Headingley 1981 were merely a desperate attempt to stimulate thoughts of improbable victory.

So, having congratulated Australia on its success, what do we say to ourselves? How do we make up that lost ground? How do we develop that winning feeling, especially with the West Indies due in England in three months time?

Inevitably there will be names that disappear from the team sheet, either temporarily or permanently, and I suspect that Graham Gooch's selection policies in the coming season will be based as much upon character assessments as pure cricketing ability, a theory that Border and Simpson have already adopted successfully.

As ever, panic is not the answer. There is enough good that has come from the tour to form a basis for future planning and still time to prepare effectively for the next challenge. ”

STATISTICS

AUSTRALIA 1990-91

1990–91 ENGLAND FIRST CLASS TOUR AVERAGES

England

Player	M	Inn	N.Out	Runs	HS	50	100	Avrge	Ct/St
Lamb, AJ	8	14	1	757	154	4	3	58.23	10
Smith, RA	10	19	6	755	108	7	1	58.08	5
Gooch, GA	8	14	1	623	117	5	1	47.92	7
Newport, PJ	1	2	1	40	40*	-	-	40.00	-
Morris, JE	4	7	-	252	132	-	1	36.00	2
Gower, DI	10	19	1	578	123	3	2	32.11	3
Lewis, CC	3	6	-	181	73	1	-	30.17	3
Stewart, AJ	9	17	-	497	95	4	-	29.24	10/-
Atherton, MA	11	22	2	577	114	2	2	28.85	10
DeFreitas, PAJ	4	8	1	139	54	1	-	19.86	-
Larkins, W	6	12	-	205	64	2	-	17.08	4
Russell, RC	8	13	1	168	36	-	-	14.00	27/4
Small, GC	9	14	3	147	37*	-	-	13.36	8
Bicknell, MP	4	6	2	28	17	-	-	7.00	2
Fraser, ARC	5	8	1	48	24	-	-	6.86	2
Malcolm, DE	10	14	2	52	18	-	-	4.33	3
Tufnell, PCR	8	10	7	13	8	-	-	4.33	6
Hemmings, EE	3	5	-	19	13	-	-	3.80	2

Player	M	Overs	Mdns	Runs	Wkts	Avrge	5WI	10WIM	Best
Hemmings, EE	3	164.0	46	391	15	26.07	-	-	4–29
DeFreitas, PAJ	4	126.0	25	353	11	32.09	-	-	4–56
Malcolm, DE	10	422.4	78	1269	39	32.54	1	-	7–74
Tufnell, PCR	8	318.0	73	887	26	34.12	2	-	5–61
Fraser, ARC	5	237.0	51	596	17	35.06	1	-	6–82
Small, GC	9	277.0	63	774	19	40.74	-	-	4–38
Gooch, GA	8	33.0	8	90	2	45.00	-	-	1–23
Bicknell, MP	4	120.4	22	409	9	45.44	-	-	3–124
Atherton, MA	11	79.1	10	330	6	55.00	-	-	3–27
Lewis, CC	3	93.0	8	342	6	57.00	-	-	3–29
Newport, PJ	1	20.0	-	78	1	78.00	-	-	1–56

1990–91 TEST SERIES: CAREER TEST AVERAGES

Australia

Player	Debut	M	Inn	N/Out	Runs	HS	50	100	Avrge	Ct/St
Alderman, TM	1981	40	51	21	203	26*	-	-	6.77	26
Boon, DC	1984–85	53	97	9	3716	200*	17	9	42.23	53
Border, AR	1978–79	120	206	37	8982	205*	51	23	53.15	129
Healy, IA	1988–89	26	36	2	704	69*	2	-	20.71	79/2
Hughes, MG	1985–86	27	33	5	493	72*	2	-	17.61	11
Jones, DM	1983–84	39	66	8	2800	216*	10	9	48.28	23
Marsh, GR	1985–86	41	76	6	2443	138*	12	4	34.90	31
Matthews, GRJ	1983–84	26	41	8	1384	130*	6	4	41.94	14
McDermott, CJ	1984–85	26	35	4	406	42*	-	-	13.10	6
Rackemann, CG	1982–83	12	14	4	53	15*	-	-	5.30	2
Reid, BA	1985–86	22	27	12	88	13*	-	-	5.87	3
Taylor, MA	1988–89	20	37	3	1831	219*	10	6	53.85	28
Waugh, ME	1990–91	2	3	-	187	138*	-	1	62.33	1
Waugh, SR	1985–86	42	64	10	2065	177*	13	3	38.24	31

England

Player	M	Balls	Mdns	Runs	Wkts	Avrge	WII	WIM	Best	Stk/Rt	RPO
Alderman, TM	40	10045	428	4511	169	26.69	14	1	6–47	59.44	2.69
Boon, DC	53	12	1	5	-	-	-	-	-	-	2.50
Border, AR	120	2887	141	1104	30	36.80	1	1	7–46	96.23	2.29
Hughes, MG	27	6135	257	3028	103	29.40	5	1	8–87	59.56	2.96
Jones, DM	39	174	14	55	1	55.00	-	-	1–5	174.00	1.90
Matthews, GRJ	26	4514	191	2129	46	46.28	2	1	5–103	98.13	2.83
McDermott, CJ	26	5613	143	3095	98	31.58	5	1	8–97	57.28	3.31
Rackemann, CG	12	2719	132	1137	39	29.15	3	1	6–86	69.72	2.51
Reid, BA	22	5132	208	2268	89	25.48	2	1	7–51	57.66	2.65
Waugh, ME	2	36	1	26	-	-	-	-	-	-	4.33
Waugh, SR	42	3866	152	1890	44	42.95	2	-	5–69	87.86	2.93

Player	Debut	M	Inn	N/Out	Runs	HS	50	100	Avrge	Ct/St
Atherton, MA	1989	13	25	1	1087	151*	7	3	45.29	12
DeFreitas, PAJ	1986–87	20	31	2	378	45*	-	-	13.03	5
Fraser, ARC	1989	11	14	1	88	29*	-	-	6.77	1
Gooch, GA	1975	85	155	5	6336	333*	37	13	42.24	88
Gower, DI	1978	114	199	16	8081	215*	38	18	44.16	73
Hemmings, EE	1982	16	21	4	383	95*	2	-	22.53	5
Lamb, AJ	1982	70	124	10	4176	139*	16	13	36.63	66
Larkins, W	1979–80	13	25	1	493	64*	3	-	20.54	8
Lewis, CC	1990	4	5	-	70	32*	-	-	14.00	5
Malcolm, DE	1989	16	21	7	90	15*	-	-	6.43	1
Morris, JE	1990	3	5	2	71	32*	-	-	23.67	2
Newport, PJ	1988	3	5	1	110	40*	-	-	27.50	1
Russell, RC	1988	20	31	6	767	128*	3	1	30.68	57/6
Small, GC	1986	17	24	7	263	59*	1	-	15.47	9
Smith, RA	1988	23	44	10	1635	143*	12	4	48.09	11
Stewart, AJ	1989–90	12	23	1	541	91*	3	-	24.59	14/-
Tufnell, PCR	1990–91	4	6	4	13	8*	-	-	6.50	1

Player	M	Balls	Mdns	Runs	Wkts	Avrge	WII	WIM	Best	Stk/Rt	RPO
Atherton, Ma	13	366	11	282	1	282.00	-	-	1–60	366.00	4.62
DeFreitas, PAJ	20	4231	139	2031	48	42.31	2	-	5–53	88.15	2.88
Fraser, ARC	11	3118	118	1255	47	26.70	4	-	6–82	66.34	2.42
Gooch, GA	85	1941	93	786	17	46.24	-	-	2–12	114.18	2.43
Gower, DI	114	36	-	20	1	20.00	-	-	1–1	36.00	3.33
Hemmings, EE	16	4437	207	1825	43	42.44	1	-	6–58	103.19	2.47
Lamb, AJ	70	30	2	23	1	23.00	-	-	1–6	30.00	4.60
Lewis, CC	4	726	16	466	12	38.83	-	-	3–29	60.50	3.85
Malcolm, DE	16	3949	118	2113	58	36.43	3	1	6–77	68.09	3.21
Newport, PJ	3	669	18	417	10	41.70	-	-	4–87	66.90	3.74
Small, GC	17	3927	154	1871	55	34.02	2	-	5–48	71.40	2.86
Tufnell, PCR	4	840	45	345	9	38.33	1	-	5–61	93.33	2.46

1990–91 TEST SERIES: AUSTRALIA/ENGLAND TEST AVERAGES

Australia

Player	M	Inn	N.Out	Runs	HS	50	100	Avrge	Ct/St
Boon, DC	5	9	2	530	121*	3	1	75.71	4
Matthews, GRJ	5	7	2	353	128*	2	1	70.60	1
McDermott, CJ	2	2	1	67	42*	-	-	67.00	-
Waugh, ME	2	3	-	187	138*	-	1	62.33	1
Border, AR	5	7	1	281	83*	3	-	46.83	4
Marsh, GR	5	10	3	314	79*	3	-	44.86	5
Healy, IA	5	7	-	175	69*	1	-	25.00	24/-
Taylor, MA	5	10	1	213	67*	2	-	23.67	8
Jones, DM	5	7	-	163	60*	1	-	23.29	4
Waugh, SR	3	4	-	82	48*	-	-	20.50	1
Alderman, TM	4	5	2	34	26*	-	-	11.33	4
Hughes, MG	4	5	-	44	30*	-	-	8.80	3
Rackemann, CG	1	2	-	10	9*	-	-	5.00	-
Reid, BA	4	5	2	13	5*	-	-	4.33	1

Player	M	Overs	Mdns	Runs	Wkts	Avrge	5WII	10WIM	NB	W	Best
158Reid, BA	4	180.1	49	432	27	16.00	2	1	12	-	7–51
McDermott, CJ	2	97.4	12	360	18	20.00	2	1	25	-	8–97
Hughes, MG	4	142.1	38	365	15	24.33	-	-	12	1	4–37
Alderman, TM	4	148.5	33	428	16	26.75	1	-	13	-	6–47
Mathews, GRJ	5	169.0	51	422	7	60.29	-	-	2	-	3–40
Border, AR	5	28.0	6	82	1	82.00	-	-	-	-	1–37
Waugh, SR	3	38.0	15	90	1	90.00	-	-	-	-	1–7
Waugh, ME	2	6.0	1	26	-	-	-	-	1	1	-
Rackemann, CG	1	28.5	5	109	-	-	-	-	-	-	-

England

Player	M	Inn	N/Out	Runs	HS	50	100	Avrge	Ct/St
Gooch, GA	4	8	-	426	117*	4	1	53.25	6
Gower, DI	5	10	1	407	123*	1	2	45.22	1
Newport, PJ	1	2	1	40	40*	-	-	40.00	-
Lamb, AJ	3	6	-	195	91*	2	-	32.50	2
Atherton, MA	5	10	1	279	105*	1	1	31.00	5
Smith, RA	5	10	2	238	58*	2	-	29.75	3
Larkins, W	3	6	-	141	64*	2	-	23.50	1
Stewart, AJ	5	10	-	224	91*	2	-	22.40	8/-
Russell, RC	3	5	1	77	30*	-	-	19.25	9/1
Lewis, CC	1	2	-	34	20*	-	-	17.00	1
DeFreitas, PAJ	3	6	1	77	45*	-	-	15.40	-
Small, GC	4	6	1	42	15*	-	-	8.40	4
Tufnell, PCR	4	6	4	13	8*	-	-	6.50	1
Fraser, ARC	3	5	-	27	24*	-	-	5.40	1
Malcolm, DE	5	7	1	27	7*	-	-	4.50	-
Hemmings, EE	1	1	-	0	0*	-	-	0.00	1

Player	M	Overs	Mdns	Runs	Wkts	Avrge	5WII	10WIM	NB	W	Best
Lewis, CC	1	15.0	-	58	3	19.33	-	-	10	-	3–29
Fraser, ARC	3	143.0	31	311	11	28.27	1	-	16	-	6–82
DeFreitas, PAJ	3	113.0	22	318	10	31.80	-	-	3	-	4–56
Hemmings, EE	1	73.0	16	199	6	33.17	-	-	-	-	3–94
Gooch, GA	4	23.0	5	69	2	34.50	-	-	1	1	1–23
Tufnell, PCR	4	140.0	45	345	9	38.33	1	-	3	1	5–61
Malcolm, DE	5	223.5	42	665	16	41.56	-	-	21	2	4–128
Small, GC	4	149.0	33	424	9	47.11	-	-	2	6	3–34
Newport, PJ	1	20.0	-	78	1	78.00	-	-	6	-	1–56
Atherton, MA	5	15.0	2	70	-	-	-	-	-	-	-

1990-91 WORLD SERIES

1 Australia v. New Zealand
Sydney Cricket Ground
29 November 1990
Toss: New Zealand
Twelfth men: TM Alderman (Australia); GE Bradburn (New Zealand)

Australia: 9-236 (43.5) (GR Marsh 46, ME Waugh 40. C Pringle 3-39)
New Zealand: 7-174 (40.0) (KR Rutherford 33, IDS Smith 33. BA Reid 2-18)

Result: Australia won by 61 runs
Man of the Match: AR Border (Australia)
Attendance: 21,359

2 England v. New Zealand
Adelaide Oval
1 December 1990
Toss: England Twelfth men: AJ Stewart (England); GE Bradburn (New Zealand)

New Zealand: 6-199 (40.0) (JG Wright 67, KR Rutherford 50)
England: 9-192 (40.0) (JE Morris 63*, AJ Lamb 49. C Pringle 3-36)

Result: New Zealand won by 7 runs
Man of the Match: JG Wright (New Zealand)
Attendance 4,650

3 Australia v. New Zealand
Adelaide Oval
2 December 1990
Toss: New Zealand
Twelfth men: BA Reid (Australia); GE Bradburn (New Zealand)

New Zealand: 7-208 (50.0) (MD Crowe 50, KR Rutherford 40, RT Latham 36*)
Australia: 4-210 (47.0) (AR Border 55, GR Marsh 45, DM Jones 38)

Result: Australia won by 6 wickets
Man of the Match: AR Border (Australia)
Attendance: 17,028

4 England v. New Zealand
WACA Ground, Perth
7 December 1990
Toss: New Zealand
Twelfth men: H Morris (England); GE Bradburn (New Zealand)

New Zealand: 158 (49.2) (MD Crowe 37, AH Jones 26. CC Lewis 3-26)
England: 6-161 (43.5) (W Larkins 44, JE Morris 31, AJ Stewart 29*)

Result: England won by 4 wickets
Man of the Match: AJ Stewart (England)
Attendance: 8,230

5 Australia v. England
WACA Ground, Perth
9 December 1990
Toss: England
Twelfth men: TM Moody (Australia); MA Atherton (England)

England: 9-192 (50.0) (AJ Stewart 41, W Larkins 38, RA Smith 37, MP Bicknell 31*. SP O'Donnell 4-45)
Australia: 4-193 (41.0) (DM Jones 63*, DC Boon 38, GR Marsh 37)

Result: Australia won by 6 wickets
Man of the Match: DM Jones (Australia)
Attendance: 24,823

6 Australia v. New Zealand
Melbourne Cricket Ground
11 December 1990
Toss: New Zealand
Twelfth men: CG Rackemann (Australia); CZ Harris (New Zealand)

Australia: 7-263 (50.0) (SP O'Donnell 66, DM Jones 54, GR Marsh 51)
New Zealand: 8-224 (50.0) (MD Crowe 81, KR Rutherford 37. ME Waugh 3-20)

Result: Australia won by 39 runs
Man of the Match: SP O'Donnell (Australia)
Attendance: 39,038

7 England v. New Zealand
Sydney Cricket Ground
13 December 1990
Toss: New Zealand
Twelfth men: H Morris (England); GR Larsen (New Zealand)

England: 194 (46.4) (AJ Lamb 72, AJ Stewart 42. C Pringle 4-35)
New Zealand: 161 (48.1) (MD Crowe 76. CC Lewis 4-35)

Result: England won by 33 runs
Man of the Match: AJ Lamb (England)
Attendance: 10,235

8 England v. New Zealand
Brisbane Cricket Ground
15 December 1990
Toss: New Zealand
Twelfth men: H Morris (England); GE Bradburn (New Zealand)

England: 6-203 (50.0) (GA Gooch 48, RA Smith 41, AJ Stewart 30*)
New Zealand: 2-204 (44.3) (MD Crowe 78, JG Wright 54, AH Jones 41*)

Result: New Zealand won by 8 wickets
Man of the Match: MD Crowe (New Zealand)
Attendance: 6,024

9 Australia v. England

Brisbane Cricket Ground
16 December 1990
Toss: Australia
Twelfth men: TM Alderman (Australia); H Morris (England)

Australia: 5-283 (50.0) (DM Jones 145, GR Marsh 82. PAJ DeFreitas 3-57)
England: 7-246 (50.0) (PAJ DeFreitas 49*, GA Gooch 41, AJ Stewart 40. GRJ Matthews 3-54)

Result: Australia won by 37 runs
Man of the Match: DM Jones (Australia)
Attendance: 20,542

10 Australia v. New Zealand
Bellerive Oval, Hobart
18 December 1990
Toss: Australia
Twelfth men: CG Rackemann (Australia); GE Bradburn (New Zealand)

New Zealand: 6-194 (50.0) (BA Young 41*, RT Latham 38, JG Wright 37)
Australia: 193 (50.0) (GR Marsh 61, DM Jones 25)

Result: New Zealand won by 1 run
Man of the Match: BA Young (New Zealand)
Attendance: 11,086

11 Australia v. England
Sydney Cricket Ground
1 January 1991
Toss: England
Twelfth men: MA Taylor (Australia); MP Bicknell (England)

Australia: 7-221 (50.0) (SP O'Donnell 71*, ME Waugh 62. ARC Fraser 3-28, PCR Tufnell 3-40)
England: 153 (45.5) (W Larkins 40, GA Gooch 37. PL Taylor 3-27, AR Border 3-24)

Result: Australia won by 68 runs
Man of the Match: PL Taylor (Australia)
Attendance: 36,838

12 Australia v. England
Melbourne Cricket Ground
10 January 1990
Toss: Australia
Twelfth men: MA Taylor (Australia); MA Atherton (England)

Australia: 6-222 (50.0) (SR Waugh 65*, IA Healy 50*, DC Boon 42)
England: 9-219 (50.0) (AJ Stewart 55, ARC Fraser 38*, GA Gooch 37. ME Waugh 4-37)

Result: Australia won by 3 runs
Man of the Match: IA Healy (Australia)
Attendance: 56,667

13 Australia v. New Zealand
Sydney Cricket Ground
13 January 1991
Toss: New Zealand
Twelfth men: CG Rackemann (Australia); CZ Harris (New Zealand)

New Zealand: 7-199 (50.0) (AH Jones 43, MD Crowe 35. ME Waugh 3-29)
Australia: 4-202 (49.1) (GR Marsh 70, DM Jones 49, MA Taylor 41)

Result: Australia won by 6 wickets
Attendance: 35,703

14 Australia v. New Zealand
Melbourne Cricket Ground
15 January 1991
Toss: New Zealand
Twelfth men: CG Rackemann (Australia); CZ Harris (New Zealand)

New Zealand: 6-208 (50.0) (RB Reid 64, AH Jones 51. SP O'Donnell 3-43)
Australia: 3-209 (45.3) (DM Jones 76, MA Taylor 71, DC Boon 40*)

Result: Australia won by 7 wickets
Man of the Finals: MA Taylor (Australia)
Man of the Series: SP O'Donnell (Australia)
Attendance: 48,957

ENGLAND TOUR MATCHES

1 Western Australian Cricket Association President's XI v. England XI,
Lilac Hill, Perth (25 October 1990)

WACA President's XI: 7-205 (TM Moody 100*, MRJ Veletta 30. CC Lewis 3-37); England XI: 4-206 (AJ Stewart 70*, DI Gower 33. CD Mack 2-29)
England XI won by 6 wickets

2 Western Australian Country XI v. England XI
Wonthella Park, Geraldton (27 - 28 October 1990)

England XI: 8d-197 (W Larkins 55, MA Atherton 40, AJ Lamb 37. M Obst 4-36); WA Country XI: 181 (P Shine 43, B Woods 40, T Waldron 35. MA Atherton 3-46); England XI: 4-121 (GA Gooch 47)
Match drawn

3 Western Australian Invitation XI v. England XI
WACA Ground, Perth (30 October 1990)

England XI: 180 (AJ Lamb 50, RC Russell 31. CD Mack 3-51); WA Invitation XI: 7-181 (DS Lehmann 50, ME Waugh 36. MP Bicknell 3-43)
WA Invitation XI won by 3 wickets

4 Western Australia v. England XI
WACA Ground, Perth (2 - 5 November 1990)

Western Australia: 289 (TM Moody 108, KH MacLeay 63, WS Andrews 31. MA Atherton 3-27, GC Small 3-59); England XI: 246 (AJ Lamb 84, RA Smith 41. CD Matthews 5-66); Western Australia: 4d-329 (GR Marsh 151, MRJ Veletta 77); England XI: 9-222 (RA Smith 98*. TM Alderman 3-49)
Match drawn

5 South Australian Country XI v. England XI
Memorial Oval, Port Pirie (7 November 1990)

England XI: 7-239 (W Larkins 110, MA Atherton 36, JE Morris 30. S Fuchs 3-84); SA Country XI: 128 (C Richards 57. MP Bicknell 3-24, PCR Tufnell 3-41)
England XI won by 111 runs

6 South Australia v. England XI
Adelaide Oval, Adelaide (9 - 12 November 1990)

South Australia: 9d-431 (GA Bishop 154, PC Nobes 131, PR Sleep 71*. MP Bicknell 3-124); England XI: 217 (CC Lewis 44, AJ Stewart 41, RC Russell 36, W Larkins 31); England XI: 325 (AJ Stewart 92, CC Lewis 73, DI Gower 56, MA Atherton 40. DJ Hickey 5-83); South Australia: 4-112 (PC Nobes 32, DW Hookes 26)
South Australia won by 6 wickets

7 Tasmania v. England XI
Bellerive Oval, Hobart (14 November 1990)

Tasmania: 6-173 (DM Wellham 63, MG Farrell 36. CC Lewis 3-36); England XI: 2-175 (MA Atherton 88*, DI Gower 30)
England XI won by 8 wickets

8 Australian XI v. England XI
Bellerive Oval, Hobart (16 - 19 November 1990)

England XI: 340 (AJ Lamb 154, AJ Stewart 95, RA Smith 71. CD Matthews 6-71, CJ McDermott 4-70); Australian XI: 192 (DC Boon 67. DE Malcolm 7-74); England XI: 4d-192 (AJ Lamb 105, RA Smith 58*); Australian XI: 6-214 (DC Boon 108. ARC Fraser 3-75)
Match drawn

9 Australian Institute of Sport Cricket Academy v. England XI)
St Peter's College, Adelaide (29 November 1990

AIS Cricket Academy: 95 (GC Small 3-7, DE Malcolm 3-13); England XI: 5-96 (RA Smith 25, W Adlam 2-18)
England XI won by 5 wickets

10 Australian Institute of Sport Cricket Academy v. England XI
St Peter's College, Adelaide (30 November 1990)

England XI: 6-237 (JE Morris 63, RA Smith 37); AIS Cricket Academy: 87 (D Martyn 32. MP Bicknell 4-30, PCR Tufnell 3-11)
England XI won by 150 runs

11 Bradman's XI v. England XI
Bradman Oval, Bowral (11 December 1990)

England XI: 7-229 (AJ Lamb 55, AJ Stewart 53*, H Morris 50); Bradman's XI: 3-231 (DS Lehmann 112*, JC Young 55, MG Bevan 51*)
Bradman's XI won by 7 wickets

12 Prime Minister's XI v. England XI
Manuka Oval, Canberra (4 December 1990)

PM's XI: 9-226 (AR Border 55*, CJ McDermott 39, PCR Tufnell 3-40) ; England XI: 9-195 (W Larkins 34, JE Morris 30, C J McDermott 3-41).
PM's XI won by 31 runs

13 Victoria v. England XI
Eastern Oval, Ballarat (20 - 23 December 1990)

Victoria: 7d-441 (WG Ayres 139, DM Jones 110, GM Watts 65); England XI: 6d-353 (AJ Lamb 143, AJ Stewart 73, RA Smith 71*); Victoria: 7d-215 (MG Hughes 64*, WG Ayres 53, JD Siddons 50. DE Malcolm 4-62); England XI: 7-204 (RA Smith 56*, DI Gower 54. PW Jackson 4-62)
Match drawn

14 New South Wales v. England XI
Lavington Sports Club Oval, Albury (13 - 16 January 1991)

England XI: 164 (PAJ DeFreitas 54); NSW: 321 (GS Milliken 107, PA Emery 53*. EE Hemmings 4-85, PCR Tufnell 4-97); England XI: 235 (MA Atherton 114, GC Small 34. GRJ Matthews 4-77, AE Tucker 4-89); NSW: 4-79 (TH Bayliss 22. EE Hemmings 4-29)
NSW won by 6 wickets

15 Queensland v. England XI
Carrara Oval, Gold Coast (19 - 22 January 1991)

Queensland: 286 (SG Law 73, IA Healy 56, CJ McDermott 50*. PCR Tufnell 5-108); England XI: 430 (JE Morris 132, RA Smith 108, GA Gooch 93, AJ Lamb 55); Queensland: 175 (SG Law 44, IA Healy 37. GC Small 4-38); England XI: 0-32
England XI won by 10 wickets